FINISHES FOR EXTERIOR WOOD

Selection, Application, and Maintenance

A comprehensive guide to the painting/staining and maintenance of homes, decks, log structures, and more.

by
R. Sam Williams, Supervisory Research Chemist
Mark T. Knaebe, Chemist
William C. Feist, Research Chemist (retired)

U.S. Department of Agriculture, Forest Service
Forest Products Laboratory
Madison, Wisconsin

ACKNOWLEDGEMENTS

Several individuals and organizations contributed to the development and publication of this manual. The authors thank Peter Sotos (The Forest Products Laboratory (FPL)) for his years of field work evaluating wood/paint systems. Much of the technical background for this manual results from these field studies. We also thank Mary Collet (FPL) for her help in editing, Susan Stamm and Art Brauner (Forest Products Society) for their help in preparing the final draft and publication, Karen Nelson, Richard Paynter (FPL), and Clay Bridge (Flad and Associates) for preparing the graphics and paintings, Anton TenWolde for his help in writing the section on moisture movement in buildings, Steve Schmeiding and Jim Vargo (FPL) for many of the photographs, and the Southern Forest Products Association and Red Cedar Shingle and Handsplit Shake Bureau for supplying photographs. Some of the information in this manual was modified from a previous publication by W. C. Feist and D. L. Cassens (Purdue University).

TABLE OF CONTENTS

CHAPTER 8. REFINISHING OF WOOD

CHAPTER 9. DISCOLORATION OF WOOD AND FINISHES

INTRODUCTION

The versatility and unique characteristics of wood have permitted the extensive use of wood and wood products in North America. Knowledge of these characteristics has been gained through practical experience over thousands of years and through scientific investigations during the last 200 years. The abundant forests in the United States have made wood and wood products an important part of our cultural heritage.

Forests continue to be an abundant part of our natural resources and, on an annual basis, natural regeneration, planting, and replanting of trees continues to be greater than the amount harvested. Although changes in harvesting practices (e.g., the decrease in harvest of old-growth forests of the Pacific Northwest) are not likely to affect the overall availability of wood and wood products, the species mix and the selection of wood products has changed and will continue to change. Large logs from old-growth and/or virgin timber have been replaced by small logs from second- and third-growth forests. Composite wood products continue to replace dimension lumber. Many of these composites are panel products. Hardwoods are being used to a greater degree for dimension lumber and siding. Nevertheless, because wood is a renewable resource, younger forests, smaller logs, different species, and wood composites can continue to provide economical building material for future generations. In addition, the environmental costs of wood (measured as energy required to produce) are roughly one tenth of competitive materials such as steel, aluminum, and concrete.

Wood continues to play an important role as a structural and decorative material in today's high-tech society. The availability of wood species varies somewhat by region within the United States. Climatic conditions also vary tremendously. Consequently, wood durability, structure design, construction practices, and finish formulations also vary.

Lumber and other wood-based composites products (plywood, particleboard, laminated beams, etc.) are used for countless exterior and interior applications. Many of these wood products serve as the first defense against the degrading effects of weather. Degradation caused by sunlight and moisture can be controlled by using good design and construction practices, and the selection and application of the finish is crucial. This is especially true in the South and similar climates, where excessive moisture can quickly cause wood decay and sunlight can cause weathering.

Just as wood and wood-based materials are a structure's first defense against degradation, finishes work in concert with these wood materials to protect both the structure and the wood elements exposed to the weather. A variety of finishes can be applied to wood to retard degradation. These finishes include clear finishes, which reveal and accentuate the natural color and figure of wood; stains, which impart a rustic appearance and partially block the natural color and figure; and paints, which totally obscure the wood color and figure.

This manual describes the characteristics of wood finishes and their proper application to solid and composite wood products. It describes how manufacturing and construction practices affect the surfaces of wood products, how various types of finishes interact with the surface, and how weathering affects the wood and finished wood surfaces. Methods for selecting and applying various exterior wood finishes are presented. Finally, the degradation and discoloration of wood finishes are discussed, and methods are given for preventing these problems.

1

• •

WOOD PROPERTIES AND FINISH DURABILITY

Wood differs from other common building materials because it is a natural biological material. Its properties vary, not only from one species to another, but also within the same species. For a particular species, properties and associated finishing characteristics are usually related to growth rate. Growth rate in turn is determined by climatic factors, geographic origin, genetics, tree vigor, and competition—factors over which we currently have little control. Differences can even be expected in boards cut from the same tree. These differences depend on where the board was cut from the log (e.g., heartwood, sapwood) and the orientation of the board compared with the annual growth rings (i.e., flat-grained, vertical-grained). In addition to the natural characteristics, manufacturing characteristics are often superimposed on wood that affect the performance of finishes. For example, the application of paper overlays to wood panel products prior to finishing improves paint durability whereas mill glaze of wood siding (a condition possibly caused during planing) can lead to premature paint flaking. Understanding some of the natural characteris-

tics of wood directly relates to understanding the durability of finishes.

Natural Characteristics

The properties of wood that vary greatly from species to species are density, grain characteristics (earlywood/ latewood ratio), texture (occurrence of vessels), proportion of sapwood, and the presence of extractives, resins, and oils.

Density

The density of wood, or its "weight," is one of the most important factors that affects finish performance. Density varies tremendously from species to species (Table 1), and it is important because "heavy" woods shrink and swell to a greater extent than "light" woods. This dimensional change occurs as wood, particularly in exterior applications, gains or loses moisture with changes in the relative humidity and from periodic wetting caused by rain and dew. Excessive dimensional change in wood stresses film-forming finishes and may cause cracking and/or flaking.

The amount of warping and checking that occurs as wood changes dimensions and during the natural weathering process is also directly related to wood density. Cupping is probably the most common form of warp. Cupping is the distortion of a board that causes a deviation from flatness across the width of the piece (Fig. 1). Wide boards cup more than narrow boards, and flat-grained boards cup more than vertical-grained boards (see Fig. 7 for diagram of grain orientation). Boards may also bow, crook, or twist from one end to the other. Warping is generally caused by uneven shrinking or swelling within the board. Furthermore, checks (small cracks along the grain) may develop from stress set up during the initial drying (shrinking) or from stresses caused by the alternate shrinking and swelling during service. High density (heavy) woods such as southern pine, Douglas-fir, and oak tend to warp and check more than do the low density (light) woods such as redwood and western redcedar (Table 1).

Earlywood and Latewood

Each year, most tree species add one growth increment or ring to their diameter (Fig. 2). For most species, this ring shows two distinct periods of growth and therefore two bands, called earlywood (springwood) and latewood (summerwood). Latewood is denser, harder, smoother, and darker than earlywood, and its cells have thicker walls and smaller cavities. The proportion of earlywood to latewood varies with each growing season, but the higher the proportion of latewood, the denser the wood. The width of growth rings depends on wood species and growth rate. For a given species and growth rate, growth rings appear the most narrow in

Table 1—Characteristics of selected solid woods for painting and finishing.

Wood	Density (lb/ft³) at 8 percent moisture content[a]	Paint-holding characteristic (I, best; V, worst)[b]	Resistance to cupping (1, most; 4, least)	Conspicuousness of checking (1, least; 2, most)	Color of heartwood	Degree of figure on flat-grained surface
Softwood						
Western redcedar	22.4	I	1	1	Brown	Distinct
Cypress	31.4	I	1	1	Light brown	Strong
Redwood	27.4	I	1	1	Dark brown	Distinct
Eastern white pine	24.2	II	2	2	Cream	Faint
Ponderosa pine	27.5	III	2	2	Cream	Distinct
White fir	25.8	III	2	2	White	Faint
Western hemlock	28.7	III	2	2	Pale brown	Faint
Spruce	26.8	III	2	2	White	Faint
Douglas-fir	31.0	IV	2	2	Pale red	Strong
Southern yellow pine	38.2	IV	2	2	Light brown	Strong
Hardwood						
Eastern cottonwood	28.0	III	4	2	White	Faint
Magnolia	34.4	III	2	–	Pale brown	Faint
Yellow-poplar	29.2	III	2	1	Pale brown	Faint
Lauan (plywood)		IV	2	2	Brown	Faint
Yellow birch	42.4	IV	4	2	Light brown	Faint
Gum	35.5	IV	4	2	Brown	Faint
Sycamore	34.7	IV	–	–	Pale brown	Faint
American elm	35.5	V or III	4	2	Brown	Distinct
White oak	45.6	V or IV	4	2	Brown	Distinct
Northern red oak	42.5	V or IV	4	2	Brown	Distinct

[a] 1 lb/ft³ = 16.02 kg/m³.
[b] Woods ranked in group V are hardwoods with large pores, which require wood filler for durable painting. When the pores are properly filled before painting, group II applies.

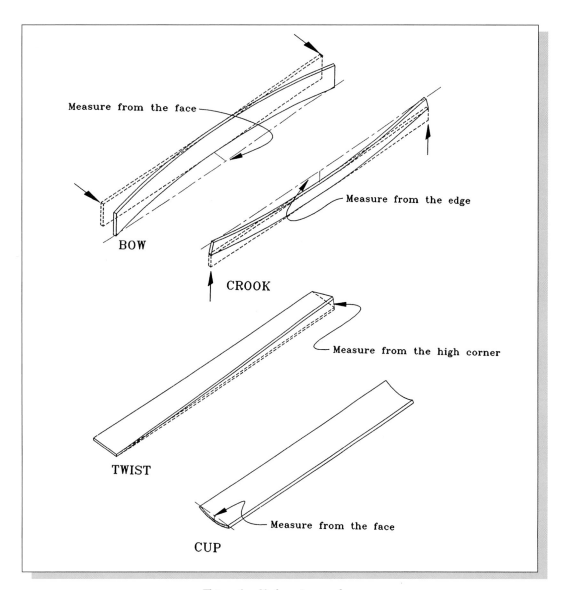

Figure 1.—Various types of warp.

vertical-grained lumber. The surface of construction and siding grades of plywood is always flat-grained and therefore growth rings appear as wide parabolic curves.

In softwood (conifer) lumber, the width of latewood bands (Fig. 3) affects paint durability and is closely related to wood density. New paint adheres firmly to newly sawn, planed, or sanded earlywood and latewood. However, moisture-induced dimensional changes in the wood can eventually weaken the paint bond, particularly over wide, dense latewood bands. The bond is further weakened if the paint becomes brittle with age. Oil-based paints are prone to embrittle with age and peel from the smooth, hard, and dimensionally less stable surface of latewood. If the bands of latewood are narrow enough, the coating may bridge the latewood and remain in place longer than it would on the wider latewood bands. Vertical-grained western redcedar and redwood have excellent paint-holding ability because of their low density and extremely narrow latewood bands. Flat-grained southern pine and Douglas-fir have dense, wide latewood bands and hold paint poorly, particularly if the wood is smooth-planed.

For hardwoods, such as oak, the durability of paint is more a function of the anatomy of the wood species and distinctions between early-

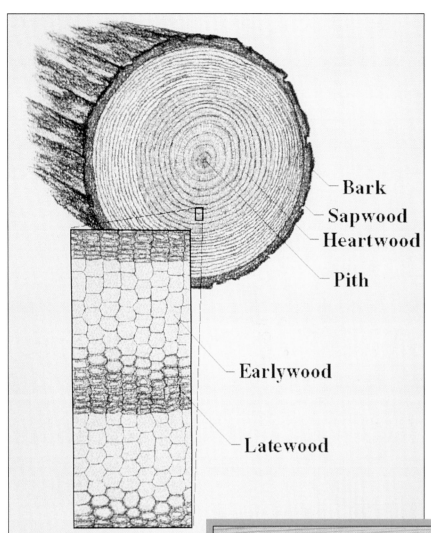

Figure 2.—*Cross section of a log.*

Bark
Sapwood
Heartwood
Pith

Earlywood

Latewood

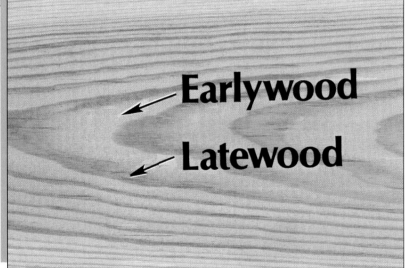

Figure 3.—Earlywood (light-colored) and latewood (dark-colored) bands in southern yellow pine. Because the difference in density between the bands often contributes to early paint failure, penetrating stains are preferable for finishing this kind of wood.

wood/latewood characteristics are less important. Unlike softwoods, hardwoods contain vessels (pores) in addition to the wood cells (Fig. 4). These vessels give added texture to the surface and may make wood from these species more difficult to finish.

Texture

Texture is often used in reference to hardwoods (Fig. 4) and refers to the general coarseness of the wood surface. Coarseness is primarily caused by the vessels, although it can also be affected by cell orientation, grain pattern, sanding, and sawing. Hardwoods are primarily composed of relatively short, small-diameter cells (fibers) and large-diameter vessels (pores). The diameter and placement of these pores give quite distinctive textures to many hardwoods and in some cases lead to finishing problems. The size and arrangement of the pores may outweigh the factors of density and grain pattern in their effect on paint retention. Hardwoods with large pores, such as oak and ash, are poorly adapted to ordinary house-painting methods because pinholes can form in the coating over the large pores. Pinholes are unsightly and lead to early failure of the coating. On the other hand, yellow-poplar has a relatively uniform fine texture, is free of large pores, and has good overall paintability in comparison to coarse-textured species.

Softwoods, in contrast, are composed of longer small-diameter cells (tracheids) and do not contain pores. The texture, much finer than that of hardwoods, is a result of cell orientation and grain pattern.

Heartwood and Sapwood

As trees mature, most species naturally develop a darker central column of wood called heartwood (Fig. 2). Surrounding the heartwood is a lighter colored cylinder of wood called sapwood. The sapwood is composed of live cells that serve to transport water and nutrients throughout the tree and provide structural support for the tree. Cells in the heartwood, on the other hand, are no longer living, and this portion of the tree serves only as structural support. Although the heartwood is not involved in the life processes of the tree, it becomes impregnated with extractives, oils, and pitch as the tree grows. Older trees have a higher percentage of heartwood than younger trees, and the amount of extractives in the heartwood seems to increase as the tree ages.

Old-growth timber from some species, such as redwood, is notable for its natural resistance to decay and insects; these species contain several unique extractives that are toxic to such organisms. The heartwood of second-growth timber is not as decay resistant as that of old-growth timber. In addition, since second-growth timber is usually smaller than old-growth timber, it contains a higher percentage of sapwood, which has little or no resistance to decay and insects.

Extractives, Pitch, and Oils

Extractives, pitch, and/or oils content of wood varies among wood species. These substances have their own properties and characteristics and are found in the heartwood of both softwoods and hardwoods. Although they con-

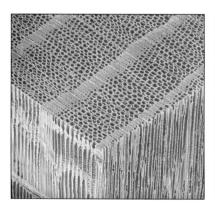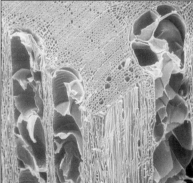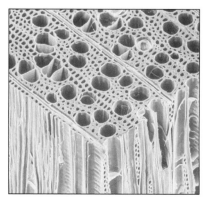

Figure 4.—Wood anatomy affects the durability of paint. Left, a nonporous wood (softwood or conifer such as southern pine); center, a ring-porous wood (white oak) showing the large open vessels characteristic of this species; and right, a diffuse-porous wood (yellow-poplar).

stitute less than 5 percent of the ovendry weight of the wood, these substances greatly affect many wood properties, including color, odor, permeability, and resistance to decay and insects. Without extractives, pitch, and oil, many woods would appear essentially identical except for their anatomical features and would lack richness in color and aroma.

Some extractives are water-soluble and are particularly abundant in those woods commonly used for exterior applications, such as western redcedar, redwood, and cypress. Such extractives are also found in lesser amounts in the heartwood of Douglas-fir and the pines. As mentioned in the previous section, the natural decay resistance of many species is attributed to the presence of extractives. However, extractives can cause discoloration of finishes. On painted wood, water and high relative humidity can leach extractives from unpainted portions of wood and deposit them on the painted surface. Water can also draw extractives through porous paint films such as latex paints. When the water evaporates, the extractives remain as a reddish-brown discoloration. This discoloration is particularly noticeable on white or very light-colored paints and solid-color stains. Excess extractives and/or oils on the wood surface can interfere with proper curing of some finishes and decrease paint adhesion.

Pitch (sometimes called resin) can be found in most softwoods, including spruce, pine, and fir, and can exude from either the sapwood or heartwood (Fig. 5). Pitch is a mixture of rosin and turpentine. At normal temperatures, rosin is a brittle solid and turpentine is a liquid. Turpentine allows the pitch to exude from the wood. Turpentine is volatile even at relatively low temperatures. By using proper kiln-drying techniques, turpentine can generally be driven from the wood, leaving behind only the solid rosin. However, different kiln schedules may be used for lumber marketed for general construction, and some turpentine may remain in the

Figure 5.—Exuded pitch from pitch pockets on lumber finished with semitransparent stain.

wood, mixed with the rosin. Although the resultant pitch melts at a much higher temperature than does the original pitch, the mixture can still move to the surface if the temperature is high enough.

If the wood surface is finished, the pitch may exude through the coating or cause the finish to discolor or blister. The most serious problems occur when the wood is heated (for example, when the wood is fully exposed to direct sunlight). Once the sticky pitch is on the surface of the wood, the turpentine evaporates, leaving beads of hard rosin (Fig. 5). Such rosin beads must be removed prior to painting or repainting.

White or light-colored paint may occasionally develop yellow or brown discoloration from the resin in the heartwood of ponderosa pine and some other pines (Fig. 6). The discoloration may diffuse throughout the coating in areas over the heartwood, leaving the sapwood area unaffected. The color comes from substances in the extractives and/or resins and is exacerbated by moisture. Discoloration can occur on wood that was damp when painted or gets wet after the paint has cured. It rarely occurs on dry wood. The problem often occurs on woodwork in the kitchen and bathroom. Because the discoloration fades with sunlight, it is less of a problem on exterior woodwork.

In some woods such as cypress, teak, and some cedars (except western redcedar), oils can cause finishing problems. The oils are mixtures of liquids or solids that can accumulate on the wood surface. They are soluble in some finishes and thus may discolor the finish. The presence of oils may also retard drying of finishes and often cause blistering, softening, and wrinkling of coatings. Some oils have high boiling points and evaporate very slowly, even at the temperatures used to kiln-dry wood. The use of correct kiln-drying schedules can reduce finishing problems. Despite potential problems with finishing, natural wood oils often provide favorable characteristics. The aromatic oils in eastern redcedar, for example, make this wood particularly suitable for wardrobes.

Juvenile Wood

The wood formed during the first few years of a tree's growth (8 to 10 years for some species) is called juvenile wood. This wood surrounds the pith, or center, of the tree. The pith can most easily be seen on the end grain of a log (Fig. 2) and sometimes on lumber (Fig. 7, b). In some species, this pith-related juvenile wood has abnormal properties and may cause large dimensional changes (generally in the longitudinal direction). These dimensional changes can cause severe warping of lumber. While mature wood does not significantly change (<0.1 per-

Figure 6.—Discoloration of finger-jointed molding caused by bleeding of resins.

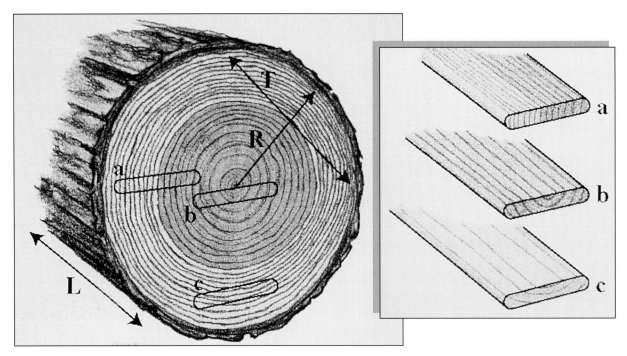

Figure 7.—Schematic of different grain orientations in log and lumber.
Tangential (T), radial (R), and longitudinal (L) directions are also shown.

cent) in longitudinal dimension between the green and dry states, juvenile wood can change up to 2.5 percent, which can result in wood shrinking more than 3 inches in a 12-foot board. With dimensional change of this magnitude, juvenile wood may split, bow, twist, cup, and/or crook, and fasteners may be pulled out.

Manufacturing Characteristics

Manufacturing processes can affect the performance of a finish on solid wood products. Finishes are affected by the way the board was sawn from the log (which determines growth ring orientation), the presence of knots and other irregularities, and moisture content.

Ring Orientation

The location from which a board is cut from a log determines the orientation of the growth rings in the piece and thus its paintability. For softwood lumber, the terms for the two extremes of grain orientation are flat-grained (Fig. 7, c) and edge-grained (vertical-grained) (Fig. 7, a). For hardwood lumber, the terms are plainsawn and quartersawn, respectively. Grain orientation may be between these two extremes (Fig. 7, b). Most standard lumber grades contain a high percentage of flat-grained boards. Lumber used for board and batten siding and shiplap siding is frequently flat-grained. Bevel siding of redwood or western redcedar is generally produced in a flat-grained standard grade and an edge-grained premium grade. Flat-grained lumber shrinks and swells to a greater extent than does edge-grained lumber and also has wider darker bands of latewood. Therefore, edge-grained lumber for siding will usually hold paint better than will flat-grained lumber of the same species and similar growth rate. Quartersawn hardwood boards hold paint better than do plainsawn boards, but the difference is relatively small compared to the difference between edge-grained and flat-grained softwoods.

Surface Texture

In addition to the "natural" texture of wood caused by its anatomical features, manufacturing processes impart surface texture to wood. These processes include the sawing and planing of lumber, cutting of veneer, and preparation of chips, flakes, particles, and fibers for composite products.

Surface texture affects and often dictates the type of finish that should be used on wood or wood products. For example, natural finishes such as penetrating stains or preservative treatments are preferred for roughsawn and flat-grained lumber. These natural finishes often accentuate the rustic look of roughsawn lumber by allowing the wood grain and surface texture to show through the finish. On plywood, paint will last longer on new rough-textured surfaces than on smooth surfaces because more paint can be applied and the film adheres better to the surface. Planed wood can be painted if the objective is to obtain a smooth, high-gloss appearance. However, the surface of planed lumber is often too smooth for good paint adhesion. Matching finish properties to wood surface properties is covered in detail in subsequent sections.

Knots and Other Irregularities

The presence of knots and other irregularities (such as bark, splits, pitch pockets, and insect damage) determines lumber grade and affects the paintability of lumber. Knots generally absorb finish differently than the surrounding wood and can affect the appearance of the finish. In pine, knots often contain a high per-

centage of resin, which may cause the paint over the knot to discolor and/or poorly adhere (Fig. 8). Furthermore, checking and cracking in large knots usually results in noticeable splits or defects. Higher grades of lumber tend to have fewer knots and are preferable for painting.

Mill Glaze

A condition known as "mill glaze" (also called planer's glaze) occasionally occurs on smooth flat-grained lumber. There is controversy over the exact cause of this condition, but many people believe it occurs as a result of planing and/or drying the lumber. The condition leads to flaking of paint, usually along the grain pattern (Fig. 9). The condition is more common in flat-grained lumber, which is more difficult to plane than edge-grained lumber. It is possible that the planing or milling process brings water-soluble extractives to the surface, creating a hard, varnish-like glaze. Excess water-soluble extractives can also form on the surface during kiln drying. The condition is often complicated by raised grain, which tends to occur more on flat-grained lumber than on vertical-grained lumber.

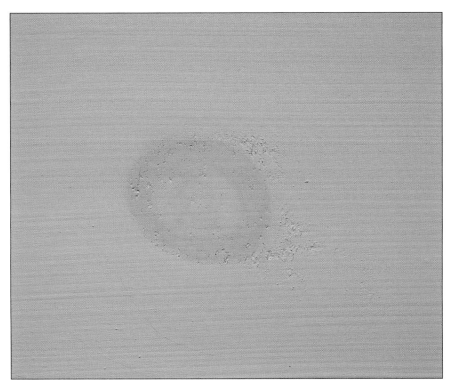

Figure 8.—Brown discoloration of paint caused by resin exudation from a knot.

During the planing process, overheating of siding may bring water-soluble extractives to the surface, creating a glaze. As these extractives age, particularly in direct sunlight, they become insoluble in water and are difficult to remove. From our knowledge of localized heating during planing and the ease with which extractives move to the surface of highly colored wood when painted, this may happen. However, it has not been possible for researchers at the Forest Products Laboratory to duplicate paint failure solely on the basis of extractives glazing at the surface.

If extractives are brought to the surface during kiln drying or any other operation prior to final planing of sanding, this final surface preparation

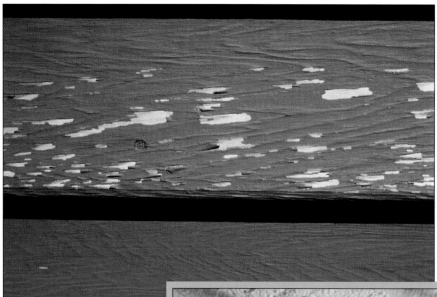

Figure 9.—Paint failure caused by raised grain and mill glaze.

Figure 10.—Raised grain on book-matched specimens of planed lumber. The cross-sections of a planed board illustrate grain-raise caused by water. Surface immediately following planing but not wetted (top); the same planed surface but wetted (bottom).

usually removes them. It is unlikely that kiln drying has any effect on the final surface of the wood, except in the case of drying degrade. If degrade has occurred, there should be obvious defects in the lumber.

As mentioned above, problems attributed to mill glaze are often complicated by raised grain. The problem is most severe on flat-grained boards because of the orientation of latewood to earlywood bands. Planer blades, particularly as they get dull, may burnish the surface and crush the less dense earlywood bands directly beneath the denser latewood bands at the surface. This crushing is more severe on the pith side than on the bark side because of the anatomical differences in these two surfaces. When these boards are exposed to weather, particularly cyclic moisture conditions, the crushed earlywood absorbs moisture and rebounds, which raises the surface latewood bands (Fig. 10). In edge-grained (vertical-grained) wood, the earlywood/latewood bands are perpendicular to the surface. This growth ring orientation makes edge-grained lumber easier to plane than flat-grained lumber, even as the planer knives get dull.

In addition to the complications caused by raised grain, the problem of mill glaze usually occurs on flat-grained siding finished with one or two thin coats of oil-based solid-color stain (also called opaque or full-bodied stain). The dry film thickness of these low solids-content finishes is about 1 mil/coat compared with 4 to 5 mils from a brush-applied three-coat paint system (primer and two top coats). The thin coatings of solid-color stain cannot withstand the stresses caused by raised grain, particularly if the coating/wood bond is weakened by build-up of extractives on the wood surface.

For flat-grained bevel siding, the simplest and best solution to the problem of mill glaze and finish failure is to install the siding rough side out. The rough side is preferable for the application of penetrating semitransparent stains; solid-color stains and paints will also last longer when applied to the roughsawn side. In addition to the lack of mill glaze, the rough side provides a better surface for finishing because it allows more build-up of the film and better mechanical adhesion. The best film build-up is obtained by brush application. If the finish is applied by roller or spray, it is advisable to back-brush the finish immediately following application to even it out and work it into the surface of the wood, thus avoiding bridging, gaps, and lap marks.

If flat-grained siding must be installed smooth side out, remove the planing stresses by wetting the surface; one or more wetting and drying cycles may be necessary to remove these stresses. Allow 2 to 3 days for the surface to dry before finishing, but the wood should not be exposed to sunlight for more than 2 weeks before application of a film-forming finish since this exposure decreases the adhesion of the coating (see Chapter 4, Weathering of Wood). Scratch sanding the surface with 50 to 80 grit sandpaper also improves paint adhesion. Sanding may also remove some of the extractives on the surface and give better mechanical adhesion to the primer.

Use a top quality three-coat paint system or apply a stain-blocking primer prior to applying solid-color stain. In selecting finishes for highly-colored woods such as western redcedar or redwood, the primer must be impervious to bleed of water-soluble extractives. Although at least one waterborne primer has been marketed for use on western redcedar and redwood, most paint manufacturers recommend an oil-based stain-blocking primer followed by two coats of top quality acrylic latex finish. Solid-color stains, particularly the latex formulations, do not block extractives very well, especially when only one coat is applied. Their performance is enhanced by priming.

Moisture Content

The amount of water contained in wood is referred to as moisture content. It includes both water absorbed into the wood cell wall and free water within the hollow center of the cell and is expressed as a percentage of dry weight. The amount of water that wood can absorb (i.e., that can be bound in the cell wall) depends on the wood species; most species can absorb about 30 percent water. The limit to which water can be bound in the wood cell wall is called the fiber saturation point. The fiber saturation point can be reached either by the absorption of liquid water or water vapor from the air.

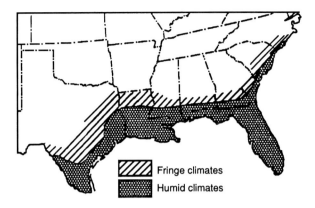

Figure 11.—Humid climates in the continental United States follow the coastal plains of the Gulf of Mexico and south Atlantic coastal areas.

Table 2—Moisture content values at time of installation for wood used in exterior applications such as siding and trim.

Geographical area	Moisture content (percent)	
	Average	Individual pieces
Most areas of United States	12	9–14
Dry southwestern areas	9	7–12
Warm, humid coastal areas	>12	9–20

The absorption of water via water vapor is rather slow compared with moisture changes that can occur through the absorption of liquid water. Liquid water can quickly cause wood to reach fiber saturation. Continued absorption of liquid water present from wind-blown rain, leaks, condensation, dew, or melting ice and snow can bring the moisture content above the fiber saturation point. As wood continues to absorb water beyond the fiber saturation point, the water is stored in the hollow centers of the wood cells. When all the air in these hollow centers has been replaced by water, the wood is "water logged," and the moisture content can be as high as 3 times the dry weight.

The amount of water vapor that can be absorbed by wood primarily depends on the relative humidity of the surrounding air. If wood is stored at 0 percent relative humidity, the moisture content will eventually reach 0 percent. If it is stored at 100 percent relative humidity, the wood will eventually reach the fiber saturation point (about 30 percent water). Of course, if kept at a constant relative humidity between these two extremes, the wood will reach a moisture content somewhere between 0 and about 30 percent. When the moisture content is in balance with the relative humidity, the wood is at its equilibrium moisture content. This balance is rarely maintained because atmospheric relative humidity is almost always changing, and as the relative humidity changes so does the moisture content of the wood. Relative humidity varies through daily and seasonal cycles, thus driving the moisture content of wood through daily and seasonal cycles. Finishes can decrease the rate of daily and seasonal moisture absorption and desorption, but the equilibrium moisture content cannot be changed through the application of finishes.

In general, the moisture content of wood exposed outdoors decreases during the summer and increases during the winter. For wood used in the interior of structures, particularly structures heated during the winter, the moisture content decreases during the winter and increases during the summer. Even in very humid areas, the relative humidity is rarely high enough for a long enough period of time to raise the moisture content of wood above 20 percent (Fig. 11). The moisture content for wood used in exterior applications varies somewhat depending on geographic region (Table 2). In the South, moisture content values can be higher than those in most areas of the United States and depend on local conditions such as coastal exposure, rainfall, elevation, and wind. However, problems associated with changes in moisture content should be minimal if the moisture content is between 9 and 14 percent. Most lumber is kiln dried to less than 20 percent moisture content before shipment. Material that has been kept dry during shipment and storage at the construction site should be close to the desired moisture content.

Plywood, particleboard, hardboard, and other wood composites undergo a significant change in moisture content during manufacture. Frequently, the moisture content of these materials is not known but they tend to have low moisture content after the manufacturing process. To improve the durability of the finish, wood composites should be conditioned prior to finishing just as other wood products.

Wood that is obviously wet and sometimes discolored may not give optimum performance. The wood will eventually dry, but shrinkage and accompanying warping, twisting, and checking can occur. If the moisture content exceeds 20 percent when the wood is painted, the risk of blistering and peeling is increased. Moreover, the dark water-soluble extractives in woods like redwood and western redcedar may discolor the paint shortly after it is applied.

So while water can enter wood in many ways, the result is always the same—poor performance of both the wood and the finish. Wood decay (rot) cannot occur unless the moisture content of the wood is near fiber saturation. This requires water. Water also causes peeling of paint. Even if other factors are involved, water accelerates the degradation of paint. Fortunately, the moisture content of lumber can be controlled. All too often, however, this critical factor is neglected during the construction and finishing processes. It is best to paint wood when its average moisture content is about at the level that is expected to prevail during the service life of the wood product. This can prevent drastic dimensional changes as the wood equilibrates to ambient conditions. The moisture content and thus the dimensions of the wood will still fluctuate somewhat, depending on the cyclic changes in atmospheric relative humidity, but the changes will not be excessive. Therefore, film-forming finishes (such as paints) will not be stressed unnecessarily and will be more durable.

Finishing Characteristics

The finishing characteristics of various softwoods and hardwoods are described in Table 1. Of the softwoods, redwood and western redcedar have the best paint-holding characteristics and are least prone to cupping and checking (group I), whereas southern yellow pine and Douglas-fir have the lowest paint-holding ability and are most prone to cupping and checking (group IV). Redwood and cedar are low density woods and have narrow bands of latewood, whereas southern pine and Douglas-fir are higher in density and have wide bands of latewood.

The best hardwoods for painting are fine, uniform-textured (small-pored) woods with medium to low density, such as yellow-poplar, magnolia, and cottonwood. These group III hardwoods should perform as well as softwoods in groups III and IV because they have less tendency to split. They do not have as great a difference in density between early- and latewood bands and therefore do not stress paint as much as hardwoods in groups IV and V. If paint fails on hardwoods, it tends to scale off in rather large flakes, regardless of the grain of the wood beneath the paint. This type of widespread failure is probably caused by the high density of certain hardwoods. Large pores in certain hardwoods can also cause problems. The pores of group V hardwoods are so large that they cannot be filled properly with ordinary housepaint. Consequently, the paint film develops pinholes that often cause early failure of the paint. To avoid this, the pores should be filled with a wood-filler paste prior to painting.

When group III, IV, and V hardwoods are exposed to the weather with inadequate paint protection, or when uneven wetting occurs, the wood has a marked tendency to warp or cup and pull away from fastenings. These hardwoods need to be attached firmly, although such nailing may cause the boards to split. Thinner boards are more likely to cup or warp from surface wetting and drying than thicker boards. For these reasons, 1/2-inch siding of heavy hardwoods is impractical. Boards for exterior exposure should be no thinner than 3/4 inch at any point and preferably less than 6 inches wide. Thick, rough (unplaned) boards, well-nailed with corrosion-resistant nails, will give the best performance.

2

CONSTRUCTION PRACTICES

In addition to choosing the most cost-effective wood product and compatible finish for a particular application, it is important to control the moisture content of the wood and follow proper construction practices during installation.

Control of Moisture Content

Moisture content of wood at the time of construction and during the life of the structure is the most critical factor affecting finish performance and susceptibility to decay and insect attack. The design and construction practices depicted in Figure 12 and listed in the shaded box (page 17) help minimize moisture damage to structures and thus improve the service life of exterior finishes.

Excessive moisture in walls and ceilings can cause mold and mildew growth, paint failure, decay of siding and structural members, and ineffectiveness of insulation. Vapor retarders were originally designed to keep water vapor out of walls and roofs and to prevent or at least minimize condensation and moisture damage from moisture diffusion into the wall. The concept of vapor retarders is approximately 50 years old,

and the original concept failed to recognize moisture carried by air flow. In the 1960s, researchers concluded that the amount of water vapor carried by air currents from air leaks could be much greater than the amount delivered by water vapor diffusion.

In the past, considerable emphasis was placed on using a vapor retarder on the interior of walls in heating climates and on the outside of walls in cooling climates. Although the vapor retarder is important, recent research has shown that the infiltration of air is much more important than the vapor retarder *per se*. That is, a vapor retarder without an air barrier has little effect. In many cases, a vapor retarder will function as an air barrier as well. For example, 6-mil polyethylene that is installed to prevent air movement will act as both an air barrier and moisture retarder. The vapor retarder must be continuous, especially if it also functions as the main air barrier in the wall or ceiling. Breaks in the vapor retarder for plumbing pipes, electrical outlets and switches, and heating/cooling vents must be completely sealed. Vapor retarder flanges should be stapled to the front face of the

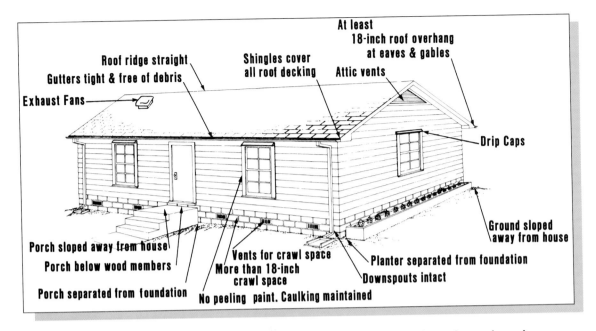

Figure 12.—*Good construction practices prevent excessive build-up of moisture in wood members. Maintaining the correct moisture content in wood increases the service life of finishes and decreases the risk of wood decay. Vents for crawlspaces are optional. (See discussion on page 18.)*

Figure 13.—*Mildew and leaching of extractives caused by rainwater splash.*

Construction practices to minimize moisture damage

1. Wide roof overhangs will provide some protection from sun and rain to at least the upper portions of the structure. A 4-foot-wide overhang protects approximately two-thirds of the siding on a conventional one-story structure from direct sunlight.

2. Metal flashings under shingles at roof edges can prevent wetting of decking and siding, particularly on roofs with a low slope.

3. Metal flashings in roof valleys, junctions of roofs and walls, along dormers, between breaks in siding (such as the horizontal juncture of panel products), and around chimneys, as well as drip caps over window and door frames, help prevent water entry.

4. Properly maintained gutters and downspouts can prevent overflow and subsequent wetting of house eaves and "rainwater splash" of the siding near ground level (Fig. 13).

5. Adequate insulation and ventilation of attics and crawlspaces can prevent moisture condensation and high moisture contents in the remainder of the structure.

6. Exhaust fans should be used to remove moisture from high-humidity areas such as baths and kitchen areas. The fans are vented to the outside of the structure. Clothes dryers should not be vented to the inside living quarters or to the crawlspace, basement, or attic. Plumbing should be well maintained.

7. For a house built on a crawlspace, the soil and the floor joists should be separated by a clearance of at least 18 inches. The ground should be covered with a 6-mil polyethylene sheet or comparable vapor retarder to prevent moisture movement from the soil. The crawlspace may be ventilated, but in warm moist climates, ventilation can cause moisture problems in an air-conditioned structure.

8. Siding, sheathing, and sill-plates should be installed at least 8 inches above the outside groundline unless pressure-treated with a wood preservative.

9. Vapor retarders or air barriers should be used to minimize condensation in walls and ceilings.

wall stud, not the side. Flanges should overlap, and any torn or damaged areas should be repaired.

Foil-backed gypsum board may be used as a vapor retarder instead of polyethylene sheets. Blanket-type insulation that has an aluminum or polyethylene vapor retarder attached to one face (such as fiberglass batt) will also suffice. Kraftpaper-backed insulation is less effective than aluminum or polyethylene as a vapor retarder.

Recommendations for vapor retarders have been based on heating/cooling requirements for three climate zones (Fig. 14)[1]. Cooling periods refer to time when air conditioning or other cooling is required.

Zone I (heating climates) ≥4,000 heating-degree days[2].

Zone II (mixed climates) ≤4,000 heating-degree days; lengthy cooling periods.

Zone III (cooling climates) warm and humid; lengthy cooling periods in which there is

1) 67°F wet-bulb temperature for 3,000 hours and/or

2) 73°F wet-bulb temperature or 1,500 hours during the warmest 6 consecutive months of the year.

For additional information consult the ASHRAE[1] Handbook and the publication by Lstiburek and Carmody[3]. Only the bare essentials of this important topic are outlined here.

It is difficult to install vapor retarders in existing buildings without removing the interior walls or adding new walls. However, certain paints may have some effectiveness as a vapor retarder if applied to the inside surface of exterior walls. Two coats of aluminum paint containing leafing pigment plus two coats of decorative paint are the best for finished plaster or gypsum wallboard. One manufacturer of household paints has determined that two coats

---

[1] The ASHRAE Handbook is being revised to reflect these definitions of climate zones. [ASHRAE Handbook, Fundamental I-P Addition. 1993. American Society of Heating, Refrigerating, and Air Conditioning Engineers, Atlanta, GA.]

[2] Heating-degree day is calculated by subtracting the average daily temperature for a 24-hour period from 65°F and summing this 24-hour value over 1 year.

[3] Lstiburek, Joseph and John Carmody. Moisture control handbook. New, low-rise, residential construction. ORNL/Sub/89-SD350/1. Oak Ridge National Laboratory, Martin Marietta Energy Systems, Inc.

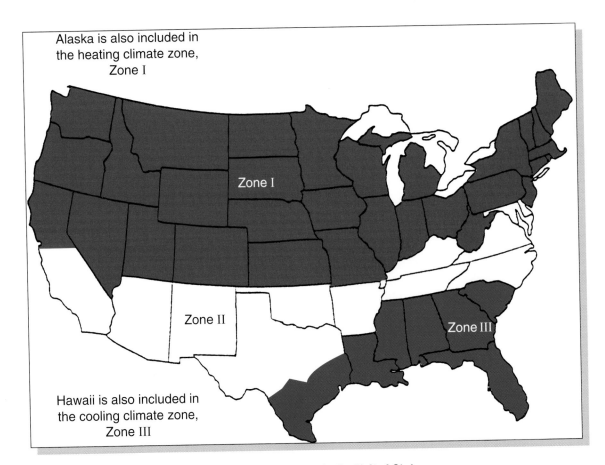

Alaska is also included in
the heating climate zone,
Zone I

Zone I

Zone II

Zone III

Hawaii is also included in
the cooling climate zone,
Zone III

Figure 14.—Climate zones in the United States.

of its alkyd semigloss interior paint, which has a dry film thickness of 2.4 mil, has a vapor permeance of 0.9. Latex paints based on butadiene-styrene resins can be used as interior vapor retarder primer paints. A reasonable rule of thumb for a minimal vapor retarder is 1.0 permeance or less. Vinyl wallcovering has a 0.5 permeance. Typical latex paints other than the butadiene-styrene paints, however, have a relatively high vapor permeance and will not effectively retard the movement of moisture through the wall. The vapor permeance for 4-mil polyethylene is 0.08 and for kraft and asphalt building papers about 0.3. Gaps in any vapor retarder decrease its effectiveness. Maintaining low indoor humidity helps decrease condensation and in northern climates (Zone I) is the most important factor for decreasing condensation in walls. The next most important factors are air barriers and then vapor retarders.

For a house built on a crawlspace, the critical factors for controlling moisture are the sep-
aration of soil and floor joists, drainage of water away from the structure, and covering of the soil in the crawlspace. In vented or unvented crawlspaces and for floors over unheated basements, blanket insulation with an attached vapor retarder is often attached to the floor joists. The vapor retarder is placed face-up toward the floor or warm side of the crawlspace. Exposed soil in the crawlspace should be covered with a polyethylene vapor retarder. When floor insulation is applied over a partially heated basement, or the house is located in a warm, humid climate, the vapor retarder may be placed face down. The crawlspace may be ventilated, but in warm moist climates, ventilation can cause moisture problems in an air-conditioned structure; the cooled surface of the flooring can condense water from the moist air entering through the vents. Water dripping from the flooring and floor joists can form pools of standing water on the polyethylene vapor retarders.

Summer air conditioning in temperate climates does not usually create serious vapor problems in exterior walls and ceilings. Normally, the cooled air is not much colder than the dewpoint of the outdoor air. Therefore, the vapor retarder should be placed in the best location for preventing winter condensation. Although condensation may occur under some summer conditions, it can be disregarded. The placement of the vapor retarder is dictated by the more serious winter moisture problems. Cooling systems should be properly designed and have the capability for adequate dehumidification of the incoming air without overcooling. Proper maintenance and operation of the air-conditioning system is important both for comfort and performance of the materials.

Humid climates deserve special attention (Fig. 11). When dwellings are air conditioned for most of the year, warm moist air can move from the outside and condense on the cooler inside portion of outside walls. This situation is the reverse of the cold weather condensation experienced in northern climates. Vapor retarders should be used on the outside of exterior walls in humid climates. Any water that gets past the vapor retarders can flow to the inside, where it can be removed by the air-conditioning system instead of accumulating in the floor, wall, or roof.

Installation of Siding

Methods for installing siding are governed by the type of siding. These methods take into consideration the properties of the siding, the dimensional changes to be expected, and the forces on the fasteners. The methods work best if the siding has been properly conditioned and stored on-site. For example, the wood should be protected from moisture and accumulation of dirt. Installation methods are described for solid wood siding and plywood and other sheet siding, and specifications are given for installing siding over rigid foam insulation.

Fasteners

The integrity of any wood structure is largely dependent on how its components are held together. Obviously, it makes little sense to properly design the wood members of a structure only to improperly fasten them together.

This section will describe the fasteners applicable for fastening siding and will provide recommendations regarding the types and sizes of fasteners.

The most common wood fasteners for siding are nails. For other wood structures such as decks other fasteners used include screws, bolts, lag screws, and various metal straps and hangers. A more complete discussion of fasteners can be found in *Wood Decks: Materials, Construction, and Finishing,* also published by the Forest Products Society.

Holding-power and corrosion protection are probably the two most important concerns when choosing fasteners. Improperly specified fasteners can loosen when wood shrinks and swells as a result of moisture cycling of the exposed wood. Not only does corrosion of steel fasteners weaken the fastener, the chemical reactions involved can also weaken the surrounding wood.

Most steel fasteners are not coated because they are intended to be used in protected environments (indoors). Obviously, if these fasteners are exposed to the weather and are not properly protected with some type of coating, they will corrode. In the mildest of cases, this corrosion can lead to unsightly staining of the wood. In more severe cases, corrosion can cause complete disintegration of the fastener and total loss of structural strength.

Several types of coatings are used to protect steel fasteners. These include paint, plastic, ceramic, and metal coatings. As the following discussion indicates, there can be considerable difference in the long-term corrosion resistance of various types of coated fasteners and their corrosion-proof counterparts.

Galvanizing is a commonly used metal coating for fasteners used in exterior environments. There is, however, considerable difference in the types of galvanized fasteners. The galvanizing (zinc, cadmium, or zinc-cadmium coating on the steel) can be applied by electroplating, mechanical plating, chemical treating, or dipping the fastener in molten zinc (hot-dipping). Obviously, the thicker the coating, the longer the protection for the fastener.

For coated fasteners, long-term exposure tests have shown that hot-dipped galvanized fasteners provide the best corrosion protection for wood that is used in damp conditions. Of course, even hot-dipped galvanized fasteners will not provide adequate performance if the thickness of the zinc coating is not sufficient. Many manufacturers coat fasteners to the standard ASTM A153, which specifies a minimum coverage of 0.85 oz/ft² of zinc. Hot-dipped galvanized nails have sufficient zinc coating to appear rough and uneven. This coating is probably thick enough for most exterior applications.

Although more expensive than hot-dipped galvanized fasteners, stainless steel is a far better option, particularly for structures that are subject to marine exposure, are in high humidity areas, and/or remain wet much of the time. Research has shown that little long-term degradation of stainless-steel fasteners occurs, even in the severest exposure conditions. Stainless-steel fasteners are available in four common grades (302, 303, 304, and 316). The higher the number, the higher the corrosion resistance (and usually the price). Grade 304 or higher is adequate for use on above-ground construction. The higher price of stainless-steel fasteners is often justified because the cost of the fasteners is small compared to the cost of the siding and the fasteners add significantly to the reliability and long-term performance.

Smooth-shanked nails often lose their holding power, when exposed to wetting and drying cycles, which can result in nail pop-up and loosening of siding boards. Although such nails are appropriate for almost all aspects of indoor house construction, deformed shank nails are recommended for fastening siding. Two commonly available deformed shank nails with the capacity to retain withdrawal resistance in outdoor use are spirally grooved and annular grooved (ring-shanked) nails.

Lumber Siding

Wood siding is relatively simple to install. It is manufactured to standard sizes in different patterns (Fig. 15) and is easily cut, fitted, and fastened in place. Courses of horizontal siding

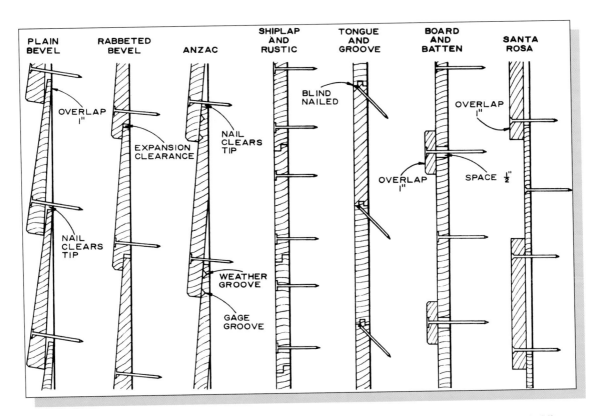

Figure 15.—Different siding patterns and recommended nailing methods for various types of wood siding. Horizontal siding patterns include plain bevel, rabbeted bevel, and anzac. Vertical or horizontal siding patterns include shiplap and rustic and tongue and groove. Vertical siding patterns include board and batten and Santa Rosa.

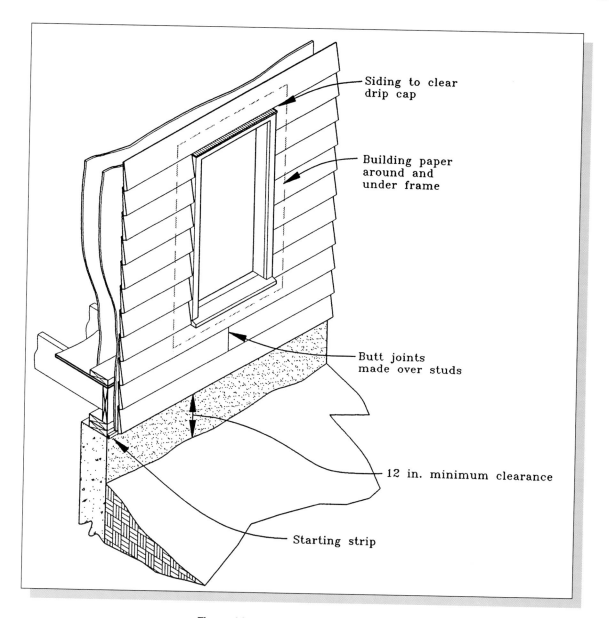

Siding to clear
drip cap

Building paper
around and
under frame

Butt joints
made over studs

12 in. minimum clearance

Starting strip

Figure 16.—Installation of bevel siding.

should be spaced so that a single board runs continuously above and below windows and doors without notching or splicing (Fig. 16). Bevel siding that is 6 inches wide should have slightly less than 1 inch of overlap between courses. Siding that is 8 inches or wider should overlap 1 to 1-1/2 inches. Enough overlap is necessary to allow for shrinkage while too much overlap causes problems with nailing. If the nails are placed too far from the lower edge of the top board, there is a tendency for the board to cup. Cupping can be a severe problem with wide flat-grained siding. If the siding is predom-

inately flat-grained, 6-inch siding has less tendency to cup than wider siding of the same thickness.

Siding should be butted squarely against door and window casings, corner boards, and adjoining boards with about a 1/16-inch gap to allow for expansion. All ends should be treated with a water-repellent preservative before caulking. Corner boards should lie flat against the sheathing, and mitered corners should be precisely fitted (Fig. 17). Even if metal corner covers are used, siding boards should be carefully cut to avoid leaving a hollow space behind them.

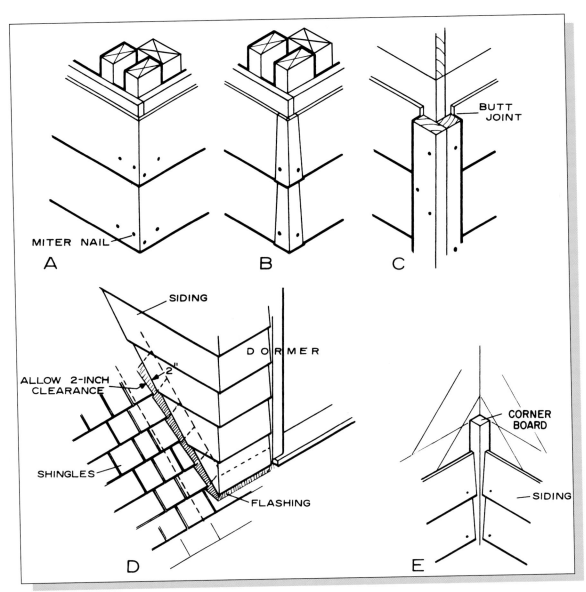

Figure 17.—Recommended procedures for corners of siding: (A) miter corner, (B) metal corner, (C) corner boards, (D) siding return at roof, and (E) interior corner.

All nailing should be driven into studs; the total effective penetration of the nail into the wood should be at least 1-1/2 inches. For example, 1/2-inch-thick siding over 1/2-inch wood sheathing requires a six-penny (6d) nail, which is 2 inches long. This combination results in a 1-inch penetration of the nail into the stud and a total effective penetration of 1-1/2 inches into the wood. An 8d (2-1/2 inch long) nail would penetrate 1-1/2 inches into the stud and provide a total penetration of 2 inches. This size of nail provides better withdrawal resistance than shorter nails. Nails that are longer than necessary should be avoided because they may interfere with wiring and plumbing. Some building codes specifically limit the length of nails to be used, particularly with 2 by 4 studs.

Hot-dipped galvanized, aluminum, stainless steel, or other noncorrosive nails are recommended. Stainless steel nails are best for naturally finished siding. Steel nails, especially the large-headed type that are designed for flush driving, often make unsightly rust spots on wood and paints. Even small-headed steel nails, countersunk and puttied, are likely to eventually cause rust stains.

For best performance, nailing patterns for various kinds of siding and application procedures should comply with the recommendations of the siding manufacturers (Fig. 15). Solid lumber siding should be fastened so that boards are free to shrink and swell, thereby decreasing the stresses that develop at the fasteners. These stresses can cause cracking and splitting.

For plain bevel patterns, the siding should be face nailed, one nail per stud, so that the nail clears the edge of the undercourse. Shiplap siding in 4- and 6-inch widths should be face-nailed, one nail per stud, 1 inch from each overlapping edge. One additional nail should be placed in the center of siding boards 8 inches or more in width. Tongue-and-groove siding, 6 inches or less in width, is either face-nailed with one 8d nail per stud or blind-nailed through the tongue. Even though the nails do not show, high-quality galvanized or other corrosion-resis-

tant nails should be used. Boards 6 inches or more in width are face-nailed with two 8d nails. For board and batten patterns, the underboards are spaced 1/2 inch apart and nailed with one siding nail at the center of the board. The batten strip, 1-1/2 inches wide, is nailed at the center with one longer nail. For board on board or Santa Rosa siding, the underboard also is nailed with one nail at the center of the board. The outer boards, positioned to lap the underboards by 1 inch, are face-nailed with two nails 1-1/4 inches from the edge. These siding patterns must be installed vertically.

Plywood and Other Sheet Siding

Exterior-grade plywood, paper-overlaid plywood, and similar sheet materials used for siding are usually applied vertically. When used over sheathing, plywood should be at least 1/4 inch thick; 5/16- and 3/8-inch-thick panels will

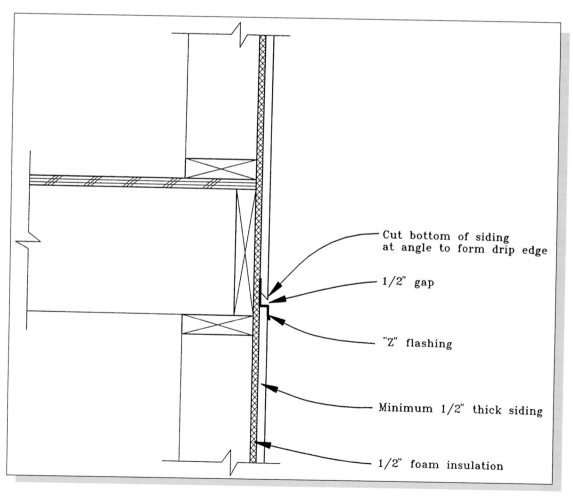

Figure 18.—Positioning of sheet siding above "Z" flashing.

normally provide a more even surface. When used as sheathing and siding, plywood should be at least 1/2-inch thick. Hardboard should be at least 1/4-inch thick, and materials such as medium-density fiberboard should be at least 1/2-inch thick. All types of sheet material should have joints caulked with mastic unless the joints are of the interlapping or matched type or battens are installed. Applying a strip of 15-lb. asphalt felt under uncaulked joints is also a good practice. When two or more sheets are applied vertically, metal "Z"-flashing should be used to protect the top edge of the lower sheet. The upper sheet should be positioned about 1/2-inch above the horizontal portion of the flashing to avoid wicking water into the siding (Fig. 18). The edges should be treated with a water-repellent preservative. A drip edge formed by a bevel cut on the lower edge can also help prevent water absorption. The top panel should *never* be placed directly on the flashing, a far too common practice.

Plywood should be nailed at 6-inch intervals around the perimeter and 12-inch intervals in the middle, although local building codes may require closer spacing. Hardboard siding should be nailed at 4- and 8-inch intervals. Always check the manufacturer's recommendations before installing any panel product, particularly with regard to the spacing between panels and specifications for nailing.

Installation Over Rigid-Foam Insulation

If rigid-foam, gypsum, or other non-nail-holding sheathing is applied under the siding, longer nails must be used to account for the sheathing thickness. Solid wood requires the same effective nail penetration as that used for lumber siding. For installing 1/2-inch wood-bevel siding over 1/2-inch rigid-foam sheathing, the American Forest & Paper Association recommends 9d smooth-shank or 7d ring-shank wood-siding nails. For 3/4-inch rigid-foam sheathing, longer nails should be used—10d smooth-shank or 8d ring-shank nails. For installing 3/4-inch wood-bevel siding over 1/2-inch rigid-foam sheathing, 10d smooth-shank or 8d ring-shank nails are recommended; for 3/4-inch rigid-foam sheathing, the nail size should be increased to 12d smooth-shank or 9d ring-shank. For installing 7/16-inch hardboard lap siding over either 1/2-inch or 3/4-inch rigid-foam sheathing, a 10d smooth-shank hardboard-siding nail is recommended.

There are many combinations of sheathing thickness, siding thickness, and nail length, but the overriding principle is quite simple—1-1/2-inches penetration into sound wood. In calculating the nail length, be sure to include any open space such as occurs with board and batten, Santa Rosa, and lap siding. Again, consult local building codes concerning electrical and plumbing clearances.

The placement of wood siding directly over rigid foam insulation may cause moisture problems. Moisture between the siding and the foam must either exit through the wood or condense and run down the lower board, causing extractives bleed. Commonly, builders place 15-lb. felt over the foam, but this just forces the moisture to migrate elsewhere. Painting the back side of the siding (backpriming) may be beneficial, however, the best solution is to fur out the siding to provide a 1/4- to 3/4-inch air space behind it. The bottom course of siding must be screened to prevent insects from entering, and the top can vent into the soffit.

A limited amount of experimental data indicates that ventilating the siding results in lower moisture levels in the siding. The *Moisture Control Handbook*, published by Oak Ridge National Laboratory, describes the rain screen design as a way to reduce the amount of rainwater entering into the walls. In addition to furring strips, a rain screen design with wood siding consists of a relatively airtight sheathing and an airspace between the sheathing and the siding that is open at the bottom and allows unrestricted air exchange with a ventilated soffit or overhang.

3

WOOD PRODUCTS USED OUTDOORS

Three general categories of wood products are commonly used in construction: lumber, plywood, and wood composites (Fig. 19). Each product has unique characteristics that can affect the durability of the finish. In addition, these products may be treated with wood preservatives or fire-retardant chemicals that can affect the finish.

Lumber

Lumber and other wood products continue to be in demand for siding, sharing the market with other materials like aluminum, vinyl, brick, and stucco. The material of choice for many architectural designs is solid wood siding, particularly bevel siding. Tongue-and-groove and shiplap patterns (Fig. 15) are also used, especially on buildings without sheathing. These kinds of siding can be applied horizontally or at an angle and tend to make the structure appear lower and longer. Vertical siding is becoming more popular. Tongue-and-groove, shiplap, board and batten, and Santa Rosa are common vertical siding patterns. The use of shiplap and tongue-and-groove siding in vertical applica-

tions requires considerable care in the selection of materials and construction. Wood that is prone to cup can form gaps in the siding. Gaps can also occur as wood with a high moisture content dries to an equilibrium moisture content. Use of furring strips over 15-lb. felt to give an air space is necessary so that the back side of the siding can dry. It is almost certain that wind driven rain will penetrate the vertical siding.

Lumber for siding and other exterior uses (e.g., window and door trim, facia, soffits) is available in a wide range of species, grades, and prices. The highest quality continues to be defect-free edge-grained western redcedar or redwood. The lowest quality siding contains knots and other defects and is likely to be primarily flat-grained. Finishes perform best on high-quality lumber.

It is possible to improve the service life of finishes, even on lower grades of lumber, by taking special care in the selection and application of finishes and by understanding the characteristics of individual boards. The service life of a finish system is determined by the lowest quality board or portion of the board. Finishes are

Figure 19.—Composite wood products commonly used in construction: (left to right) textured roughsawn plywood, particleboard, waferboard, and textured hardboard. Special precautions should be taken when painting or staining these products.

less durable on boards with a flat-grained pattern, wide latewood growth rings, and excessive knots or other defects. Boards with these characteristics should be used in areas where appearance is not important or in areas not exposed to the weather. Place low-quality boards in areas that receive little or no exposure to the sun and rain, such as close to the eaves or on the north side of the building. Paint performance can be improved by placing flat-grained siding bark-side out. The grain is less likely to raise on the bark side. If possible, use the roughsawn side of flat-grained lumber and/or siding. If the texture of the roughsawn side is too coarse for a particular use and the smooth side must be used, sand the smooth side with 50 to 80 grit sandpaper to improve paint adhesion.

Lap siding poses a special problem because the lumber has both bark-side grain and pith-side grain. Pith-side grain is prone to raise. Lap siding is manufactured by ripping a piece of dimension lumber on a diagonal to form two pieces of bevel siding. The ripped side is left roughsawn. If the original board is edge-grained, both pieces of bevel siding will be edge-grained and will not be distinguishable in regard to bark and pith. However, if the original board is flat-grained, the two pieces of bevel siding will have opposite bark/pith orientations. One piece will have bark-side grain on the smooth side and pith-side grain on the roughsawn side, whereas the other will have pith-side grain on the smooth side and bark-side grain on the roughsawn side. It is not possible to use only the bark side regardless of whether the smooth or rough side is used. Less problems will occur if the rough surface is finished rather than the smooth surface.

One effort to circumvent the finishing problems inherent with defects such as knots is the manufacture of defect-free finger-jointed lumber (Fig. 6), which is made by gluing short defect-free pieces together to form dimension lumber and/or trim. These products find widespread use for window and door trim and facia boards. Unfortunately, little care is used to match grain patterns, growth rate, or heartwood/sapwood content during manufacture. Each piece generally contains both edge-grained and flat-grained sections. Therefore, the

Figure 20.—Early paint failure on plywood caused by penetration of moisture into surface checks.

characteristics of this lumber are controlled by the lowest-quality components—the flat-grained sections—which determine the service-life of the finish system. The finish frequently fails, often within a year or two, only on the flat-grained sections; the finish on the edge-grained sections lasts much longer. Pre-selection of boards can be quite difficult, particularly with window and door units that have the exterior trim attached to them during manufacture.

For species that do not provide a good surface for paint, consider applying a non-film-forming penetrating-type finish, such as a water repellent, water-repellent preservative, or semi-transparent penetrating stain instead of paint. These products have a longer service life on roughsawn surfaces than on smooth surfaces.

Plywood

Exterior plywood manufactured from southern pine, Douglas-fir, and western redcedar is commonly available in smooth-sanded and roughsawn forms. Roughsawn plywood with vertical grooving to simulate board and batten

and other patterns is often specified for exterior use (Texture 1-11 or T 1-11). Smooth plywood is not recommended for siding, but it is often used for soffits. Both smooth and roughsawn plywood can develop surface checks (face checks), especially when exposed to moisture and sunlight. These surface checks can lead to early paint failure with oil or alkyd paint systems (Fig. 20). This problem can be reduced by using quality acrylic latex stain-blocking primer and top coats, which are more flexible than oil and alkyd systems. The flat-grained pattern of plywood also contributes to early paint failure (Fig. 21). If paint or any other film-forming finish is to be used on smooth plywood, roughening the surface with 50 to 80 grit sandpaper prior to priming should improve the life of the finish.

For painting, the best product is plywood manufactured with a medium-density paper overlay (MDO). This product holds paint quite well, but it does not accept penetrating stains. The MDO plywood is not always a stock item in many lumberyards, but it can usually be ordered. Penetrating stains can also be used for

Figure 21.—Paint failure over wide latewood bands on plywood.

exterior plywood without MDO; however, service life on smooth plywood is limited because the finish does not absorb fully into the wood.

Plywood should never be left unfinished if it is to be exposed outdoors. The natural weathering process degrades the thin surface veneer of most plywood fairly quickly (Fig. 22). Transparent finishes are also unsuitable for plywood because they do not protect the surface from weathering. Even if transparent finishes contain ultraviolet radiation stabilizers and water repellents, they do not have long service lives.

Composite Wood Products

Composite wood products are made by forming small pieces of wood or wood fibers into large sheets, usually 4 by 8 feet, or into the size required for a specialized use such as beveled siding. These products may be classified as fiberboard or flakeboard, depending upon whether the basic component is a wood fiber or a flake. Along with plywood, composite products account for more than half the total surface

area of all materials used as exterior siding for new construction in the United States.

Hardboard is a relatively dense type of fiberboard available in 4- by 8-foot sheets and in beveled siding. Its tempered or treated form, designed for outdoor exposure, is used extensively for siding. Flakeboard, a type of particleboard, is used extensively as sheathing and floor underlayment. Depending on the flake size and the panel construction, flakeboards are classified as waferboard or oriented strandboard. Waferboard and flakeboard are made from relatively large flakes or shavings. The large flakes improve the strength and stiffness of the composites compared to that of other types of particleboard. Oriented strandboard (OSB) is manufactured from rectangular flakes (strands) that are cut with the length parallel to the grain. Alignment with the grain increases the stiffness of the strands. The surface layers are oriented along the length of the board, and the center layer is perpendicular to the surface layers much like the veneers in plywood. The properties of OSB are similar to those of plywood, and OSB

Figure 22.—Front view (top) and cross-sectional view (bottom) of an exterior grade of plywood siding after 10 years of exposure. Portions of the plywood were covered with boards to give a board and batten appearance; the left portion of the board was covered.

is currently being used in many structural applications previously reserved for plywood. A wide variety of products, which differ in mechanical properties (strength and stiffness) and durability, are currently available.

Waferboard is prone to delamination of particles as well as decay when coated with non-porous (oil-based) paint systems, even when pretreated with a water-repellent preservative. This material is best suited for use as underlayment and sheathing.

Only composite wood products manufactured specifically for exterior use should be used outdoors. Film-forming finishes such as paints and solid-color stains will provide the most protection. However, finishes cannot adequately protect composite products made with non-water resistant adhesives. If the products are resistant to moisture and structurally sound, film-forming finishes further enhance their durability, particularly with regard to weathering. Some composites are factory primed and top-coated, others are only primed, and some have no finish. Some composites may be over-laid with a resin-treated cellulose fiber sheet (similar to MDO plywood) or with wood veneers. These surfaces have improved appearance and finishing characteristics. Overlaid products may perform quite well on structures designed and constructed to protect siding (e.g., roof overhang, gutters, and downspouts).

Hardboard can provide an excellent surface for finishes. However, naturally occurring water-soluble wood extractives in the wood may leach through the paint coat and discolor it. Alkyd (oil-based) or acrylic stain-blocking primers will usually prevent extractives bleed. The petrolatum used as a water repellent in some hardboard products may also cause a slight discoloration known as "wax bleed," which is usually caused by incompatibility between the water repellent in the hardboard and the surfactant in the finish. Wax bleed has seldom been a problem in recent years. Research has shown that two- and three-coat systems using acrylic latex stain-blocking primer and top-coat finishes provide good overall performance. Except when used for edge treatment (described below), pretreatment with water-repellent preservative is not recommended for hardboard because it does not absorb readily into the material. In addition, most hardboard is factory primed.

The edges and ends of all composite products tend to absorb water more readily than the other surfaces. As a result, composites will often swell in thickness. Swollen edges will not completely return to their original thickness even when they dry. Edge treatment with a water-repellent preservative prior to painting helps eliminate the tendency to swell. The water repellent works in combination with a good paint system to decrease the uptake of moisture. Priming the edges also helps eliminate moisture absorption.

Treated Wood Products

Preservative Treatments

Wood is often used outdoors where special treatments with wood preservatives are required. Wood in these situations requires protection against decay (rot) and insects. Typical examples include wood in contact with the soil or exposed to high humidity and/or water (decks, fences, furniture, wood roofs, and marine structures). In soil contact, preservative-treated wood lasts up to 10 times longer than untreated wood. Commercial pressure processes, when done according to industry

---

NOTE: The Environmental Protection Agency (EPA) has issued Consumer Information Sheets on each of the three general classes of wood preservatives: creosote, pentachlorophenol, and the inorganic arsenicals, which include chromated copper arsenate (CCA), ammoniacal copper arsenate (ACA), and ammoniacal copper zinc arsenate (ACZA). The Consumer Information Sheets are summarized in Chapter 11, Health and Environmental Considerations.

CAUTION: For items where human contact is likely or where food will be served, make certain that the wood preservative and finishing system is acceptable for that application.

standards, will provide lasting protection, provided the material is installed and used in accordance with those standards.

Lumber, plywood, and other wood products pressure treated with preservatives should be finished to protect them from weathering. However, some preservative treatments are not conducive to finishing. Each class of wood preservatives imparts certain characteristics to the wood that affect its ability to accept and retain a finish. The general classes of wood preservatives are 1) preservative oils such as coal-tar creosote, 2) organic solvent solutions such as pentachlorophenol, and 3) waterborne preservatives.

It is impossible to successfully finish wood that has been pressure treated with coal-tar creosote or pentachlorophenol in a heavy oil solvent with low volatility. The surface is generally oily and dark, and the dark color usually bleeds through the finish. By the time the wood weathers sufficiently to remove the oils from the surface, the wood is too degraded to hold paint. The weathered wood can sometimes be stained, but it is best to let it weather for a year before finishing. This is one of the few situations where lengthy preweathering is advantageous.

Coal-tar creosote and pentachlorophenol are restricted-use pesticides and are therefore not available to the general public. However, wood treated with these preservatives is still available as either new or used material, such as railroad ties and poles. The EPA Consumer Information Sheets specify that wood treated with either of these preservatives should **not** be used where frequent or prolonged contact with the skin will occur. Materials treated with these preservatives are normally intended for industrial use. Because of these restrictions, coal-tar creosote and pentachlorophenol are not commonly used in or around residential or commercial buildings.

Waterborne preservatives, such as chromated copper arsenate (CCA), ammoniacal copper zinc arsenate (ACZA), and ammoniacal copper quaternary (ACQ) are the most common preservatives used to pressure treat wood. Wood treated with waterborne preservatives is commonly available at retail lumberyards. During the treating process, the wood reacts with the waterborne preservatives to form an insoluble metal complex. It generally has a clean, paintable surface (especially wood treated by a CCA-type pressure treatment), which is characterized by a greenish or brownish color. In fact, those preservatives that contain chromium decrease the degrading effect of weathering. Although the chromium compounds in CCA give some protection against weathering, all treated wood should be maintained with a finish to protect it from the sun. Preservative-treated wood products can be finished with a wide range of products; the selection of the finish depends primarily on the type of structure. When purchasing wood containing a waterborne preservative, be certain to ask for the Consumer Information Sheet, which outlines the proper use, finishing characteristics, and disposal practices for the preservative-treated wood. Preservative treatments should be done in strict adherence with the American Wood Preservers Association (AWPA) standards, and the lumber should contain a quality stamp indicating the treatment, treating company, and inspection bureau.

The finishing properties of wood treated with a waterborne preservative depend primarily on the wood properties, not the preservative treatment. Most pressure-treated construction lumber and plywood in the eastern United States is produced from southern pine. In the western United States, preservative-treated wood species include ponderosa pine and Douglas-fir. Because of the relatively poor paint-holding properties of these three species, oil-based penetrating stains or other penetrating finishes provide better service than do other finishes. Paint adhesion and stain absorption are best on roughsawn lumber and plywood. As the demand for treated lumber increases, other species are likely to be marketed; the selection of the best finish system will still depend on wood species and use.

Wood that is pressure treated with waterborne preservatives often contains large quantities of water when shipped to retail lumberyards. Make certain that the lumber is dry before finishing. Air drying in place is acceptable, although some shrinking, warping, and checking may result. Drying may take days or weeks, depending on how wet the wood is initially and on drying conditions. See Chapter 6, Application of Exterior Wood Finishes, for more detailed information on finishing preservative-treated wood.

Pressure treatment of wood with preservatives should not be confused with treatment of wood by dipping or brushing processes using a water-repellent preservative. Window and door trim are often treated in this way, and the same solution can be brushed onto wood siding. Although these methods do not penetrate the wood deeply, they do provide some protection against decay in aboveground exposure and improve paint performance. With nonpressure processes, the preservative penetrates the end-grain of the wood but only penetrates a thin layer of the outer wood on the lateral surfaces. Therefore, surface treatments will not last long in severe applications such as ground or water contact. However, these surface treatments can be useful with wood products used in above-ground low- to medium-decay hazard areas, such as exterior millwork, siding, and above-ground parts of fences and decks. The non-pressure application of water-repellent preservatives is also useful as a pretreatment before painting.

Fire-Retardant Treatments

Wood can be treated with several types of fire retardants. There are substantial differences between fire retardants intended for use indoors and those intended for exterior applications. Some retardants used for indoor applications take up moisture readily and thus can prevent good adhesion of film-forming finishes. Blooming, the movement of the treating chemical to the surface and subsequent formation of crystals, can also occur. Fire-retardant-treated wood made for indoor applications should never be used outdoors. Only those fire-retardant treatments specifically prepared and recommended for outdoor exposure should be used outdoors. As with preservative treatments, fire-retardant treatment should be done in strict adherence with American Wood Preservers

NOTE: Creosote, pentachlorophenol, and waterborne arsenical wood preservatives are restricted pesticides and can be applied only by licensed pesticide applicators. When purchasing wood products treated with preservatives, be certain to ask for the EPA-approved Consumer Information Sheet, which outlines proper use, handling, and disposal procedures for this material (see Chapter 11, Health and Environmental Considerations).

CAUTION: The pesticides (wood preservatives, mildewcides, and fungicides) described in this manual were registered for the uses described at the time the manual was prepared. Registrations of pesticides are under constant review by the EPA. Therefore, consult a responsible State agency on the current status of any pesticide. Use only pesticides that bear a Federal registration number and carry directions for home and garden use.

Pesticides used improperly can be injurious to humans, animals, and plants. Follow the directions and heed all precautions on the label. Avoid inhalation of vapors and sprays; wear protective clothing and equipment if these precautions are specified on the label.

If your hands become contaminated with a pesticide, do not eat, drink, or smoke until you have washed. If you swallow a pesticide or if it gets in your eyes, follow the first aid treatment given on the label and get prompt medical attention. If a pesticide gets onto your clothing or skin, remove the clothing immediately and wash skin thoroughly.

Store pesticides and finishes containing pesticides in their original containers out of the reach of children and pets, under lock and key. Follow recommended practices for the disposal of surplus finishing materials and containers. Scraps of chemically-treated wood or finished wood should never be burned, either for heat or for disposal. Toxic fumes may be released.

Association (AWPA) standards, and the lumber should contain a quality stamp indicating the treatment, treating company, and inspection bureau. Because fire-retardant treatments differ, the manufacturers or suppliers should be consulted in regard to finishing details since they usually have specific recommendations for achieving maximum service life from paint and other finishes.

Treated woods are generally painted according to the manufacturer's recommendations rather than left unfinished because the chemical treatment and subsequent kiln-drying process often discolors the wood. Fire-retardant-treated lumber is normally kiln-dried to 19 percent moisture content. The treatment leaves a dry water-resistant surface, but the process darkens the wood's surface somewhat, and noticeable marks often result where the lumber contacts the small sticks ("stickers") used to separate the lumber during drying. These sticker marks normally do not weather away with exposure, and application of clear or lightly pigmented stain will not cover them. There are alternative ways to obtain a finished surface that shows the natural grain and color characteristics of the wood. For example, on special order, the lumber may be surfaced after treatment and drying, which results in a much cleaner, brighter, and smoother surface. Some manufacturers use stickers between every other layer of lumber or plywood, so that one surface remains free of sticker marks.

As with preservative-treated wood, the finishing characteristics of fire-retardant-treated wood primarily depend on the wood species. Species such as southern pine and Douglas-fir are more difficult to finish than species such as western hemlock and ponderosa pine. Quality surface preparation, application, and materials will always improve the service life of the finish.

4

●●●●●●●●●●●●●●●●●●●●●●●●●●●●●●●●●●●

WEATHERING OF WOOD

Natural weathering of wood can be considered the simplest method of wood finishing. Weathering can form a silver gray patina on the wood, which, under ideal conditions, can last for decades. Exterior use of wood dates back thousands of years, yet durable paints and other finishes became available only within the last 150 years. Prior to the mid-1800s, exterior surfaces were left to weather naturally; only later were painted surfaces used by the general populace. Recent interest in colonial traditions and furnishings as well as the do-it-yourself trend has revived the popularity of naturally weathered wood and rustic finishes (Fig. 23). Some wood houses left unfinished to weather naturally have lasted for centuries (Fig. 24).

The aesthetic appeal and life expectancy of wood and the compatibility of the wood with potential finishes are greatly affected by weathering. Weathering modifies the molecular structure of wood through a complex combination of chemical, mechanical, biological, and light-induced changes, all of which occur simultaneously and affect one another. In general, within 2 months of exposure to sunlight, all woods

turn yellowish or brownish, then gray. After the initial color change and graying, further changes are very slow to develop. Dark woods, however, eventually become lighter and light woods become darker. Subsequently, surface checks, then cracks may develop. The grain raises and loosens, the boards cup and sometimes warp, and the wood surface becomes friable, with fragments separating from the surface.

Before wood or wood-based products are left to weather naturally, two factors should be carefully considered. First, wood left to weather naturally will likely develop mildew. In warm, humid climates typical in the South, mildew may be very unsightly and blotchy. Second, wood that becomes wet, even periodically, can eventually decay. This decay should not be confused with the surface weathering process just described. Wood decay is the biological deterioration of the cellulose and/or lignin throughout the entire thickness of the board. To help guard against decay, which may take from one to several years to develop, all structures should be built so that exposure to both atmospheric and ground moisture is minimized and moisture is

Figure 23.—Houses with western redcedar siding that have been allowed to weather naturally. Top, house finished with a weathering stain after construction. Bottom, house with no finish.

not trapped. Furthermore, the naturally durable heartwood of certain species such as western redcedar and redwood or preservative-treated wood should be chosen when the decay risk is high.

Raised grain, checking, and warping are minimal with edge-grained lumber and low-density species as compared to flat-grained lumber and high-density species. Cupping can be minimized if the width of the board does not exceed eight times the thickness. Low-density defect-free softwoods tend to cup less than do the lower grades of lumber or high-density species, especially hardwoods.

Figure 24.—Some naturally weathered houses have lasted for centuries. Top, log cabin in Virginia, built in the 1850s. Bottom, New England house built in the 1700s.

Weathering Process

The first sign of the weathering process is a change in the color of the wood. The surface of light-colored woods turns yellow (Fig. 25); redwood, cedar, and hardwoods with dark heartwood appear to be bleached. This color change begins on the surface as soon as the wood is exposed to the sunlight and is relatively shallow (less than 0.1 inch in depth). With some highly colored species, color changes can occur within minutes of exposure to direct sunlight. The initial color change results from decomposition of extractives at the surface. Subsequent changes result from the decomposition of lignin by sunlight, particularly ultraviolet radiation. The sunlight-catalyzed degradation of lignin is the necessary factor for weathering. Lignin is the complex chemical structure that holds the individual cells together; it constitutes from 15 to 35 percent of the extractive-free dry weight of wood.

Weathering of wood should not be confused with decay. Photochemical degradation is manifested by an initial color change, followed by loosening of wood fibers and gradual erosion of the wood surface (Fig. 26). Rain washes the degraded wood materials from the surface.

Rain and/or changes in humidity cause dimensional changes in the wood that accelerate the erosion process. Erosion is more rapid in the less-dense earlywood than in the latewood, which leads to an uneven surface (Fig. 27). Over time, the wood surface erodes (Fig. 28), depending on the exposure, the species, and the intensity of UV radiation.

As weathering continues, the surface turns gray. This change in color is caused by two processes that may occur simultaneously. The first process is cellulose enrichment of the surface caused by the degradation of the brown-colored lignin and leaching of the extractives. The surface layer of wood develops loosely matted fibers of nearly pure cellulose. This is the classic silvery gray color characteristic of wood exposed to intense sunlight in cool climates with little rain, such as high mountains, or in coastal areas where salt is present in the air.

The other process that causes wood to turn gray results from the growth of mildew. Certain species of the organisms that cause mildew occur anywhere a sporadic supply of moisture is available; these organisms can cause the wood surface to turn uniformly gray within weeks. The organisms may also produce dark spores

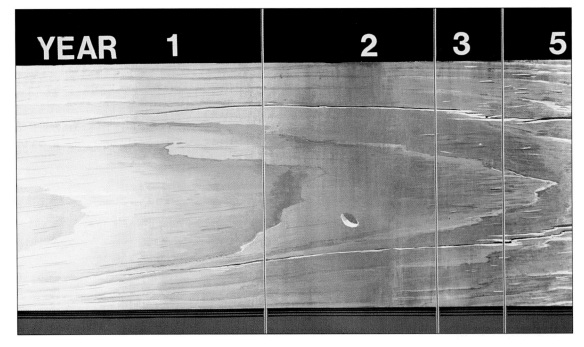

Figure 25.—Schematic of color and surface changes on a typical softwood during the natural weathering process.

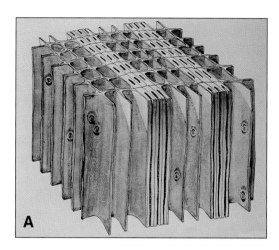 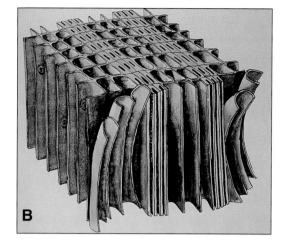

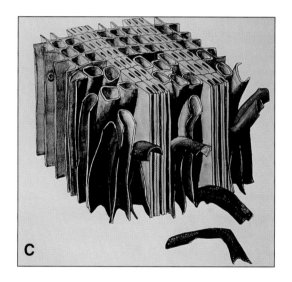 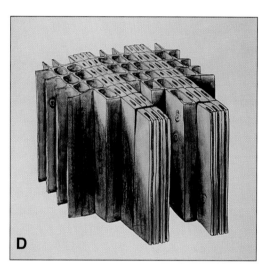

Figure 26.—Schematic of wood surface erosion by UV radiation and water. A, Unexposed wood; B, early phase of weathering showing loosening fibers; C, early phase of fiber loss; and D, later phase showing primarily loss of less-dense earlywood, leading to a "washboard" surface.

and mycelia, which can produce the dark gray/black, blotchy, and unsightly appearance of some weathered wood (Fig. 29). This is a particularly serious problem with unfinished wood in humid areas in the South. Whether caused by cellulose enrichment and/or mildew, all wood surfaces will eventually turn gray when exposed to sun and rain.

Rate of Weathering

Following the initial color change, the rate of weathering is slow and results in erosion of the wood surface. In general, for softwoods like pines, firs, redwood, and spruce, about 1/4-inch of wood thickness erodes every 100 years. The maximum weathering rate reported is 5/8-inch per 100 years for slow-grown (24 growth rings per inch) western redcedar exposed vertically facing south. For dense hardwoods like the oaks, the weathering rate is only about 1/8-inch per 100 years. The weathering rate is affected by climatic conditions, amount of exposure, wood density, amount of earlywood and latewood, growth ring orientation, growth rate, and lignin and extractives content. In general, the less dense the material and/or the more severe the exposure, the faster the weathering (erosion rate).

Figure 27.—Western cedar exposed to weather for 8 years. Top, weathered specimen with top half protected by a metal strip. Bottom, side view micrograph of weathered surface.

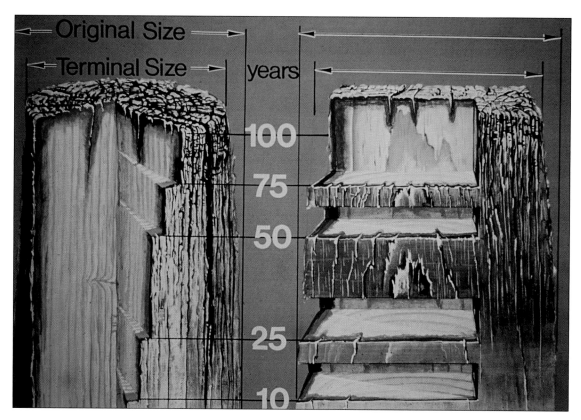

Figure 28.—Artist's rendition of surface changes in posts with more than 100 years of weathering. Bottom of posts shows early phase of weathering (slight color change and checking). Top of posts shows substantial wood loss and deep cracks.

Surface Deterioration

In addition to color changes and erosion, the wood surface is deteriorated by moisture. Water vapor is adsorbed or released with changes in relative humidity. Unprotected wood quickly absorbs rain or dew, then quickly dries in direct sunlight. These changes in the moisture content of wood cause swelling and shrinking, thus stressing the surface of the wood. Moisture, in combination with sunlight, causes macroscopic and microscopic intercellular and intracellular cracks and checks. Face-checking as well as warping and cupping can follow. Differential swelling and shrinking of earlywood and latewood can also raise the wood grain. With the sun-catalyzed decomposition of lignin, the wood surface loses strength; the added water-induced dimensional changes slowly erode the weakened surface (Fig. 30). Hail and wind-blown sand or dirt accelerate this deterioration.

Although the appearance of weathered wood is attractive for certain architectural effects, it does take time to develop. Moreover, the change caused by weathering seldom occurs evenly over different parts of a building. Those portions exposed to the most sun and rain become weathered first, usually the lower portions of the building, particularly on the south side. The top portions of the building, particularly if protected by large overhangs, porches, or other features, weather more slowly. For a year or two, or even longer in protected areas, the wood may have a mottled appearance, varying from that of freshly cut lumber to gray weathered wood. Dark brown areas from extractives in species such as redwood and western redcedar may persist even longer on wood in protected areas. The unequal effects of weathering are generally not acceptable, particularly in commercial buildings, which need to maintain an attractive appearance. If painting is being considered, weathered surfaces provide a very poor substrate for any film-type finish. Even a few weeks of exposure of a new, clean wood sur-

Figure 29.—Mildew on weathered siding.

Figure 30.—Weathered surface of unpainted southern pine after 20 years of outdoor exposure.

face will decrease its paintability and the life of the paint. On the other hand, somewhat weathered surfaces may be beneficial for penetrating finishes because they allow the wood to absorb more finish.

Wood should not be allowed to weather naturally in the South because the warm, humid climate causes rapid mildew growth, followed by moss; decay may also develop with time.

Artificial Weathering

To obtain a weathered appearance quickly, solid wood can be artificially weathered. The easiest method is to apply a commercially prepared bleaching oil, bleaching stain, or weathering stain. The oil or stain is essentially a water-repellent finish that contains some gray pigments. To maintain a uniformly gray wood surface, the bleaching oil may have to be refinished periodically. Alternatively, the finish may be allowed to wear off naturally, resulting in a more uniform, weathered appearance.

In addition to the commercially available products, wood may be treated with several different chemicals or chemical combinations to produce a weathered or aged appearance. Little quantitative information is available concerning these treatments, so some experimentation will be required to obtain an acceptable color. One relatively simple method is to coat the wood with a strong solution of tea and let the wood dry. Then, make a solution of ferrous ammonium sulfate (available from a chemical supply company), about 1 teaspoon per cup of water, and apply it to the wood (Fig. 31). Darker gray can be achieved by repeated applications or by increasing the strength of the solution.

Weathered barn boards or artificially weathered wood may be available commercially. The surface texture of artificially weathered wood is produced by rough sawing, sand blasting, wire brushing, and/or planing with notched knives or other mechanical means. Color is usually controlled by staining or chemical treatment. Caustic solutions can be used to "weather" wood; however, like naturally weathered wood, the surface is degraded.

Water-repellent preservatives or semitransparent stains can also be used to achieve a natural appearance. Water repellents or water-repellent preservatives may be used to retain the bright color of freshly sawn lumber. Those finishes containing effective mildewcides work best. Penetrating oil-based stains (available in most colors) can be applied to protect the wood and provide uniform color.

Weathering of Wood-Based Composites

Exterior use of wood-based composites such as plywood, hardboard, flakeboard, and particleboard is increasing. These materials require protection from weathering and cannot be left to weather to a natural weathered appearance as can solid wood. For example, weathering of plywood is directly related to the quality and type of the veneer and adhesives. Small checks are produced during the manufacture of plywood veneers. Exposure to the weather enlarges these checks, thereby allowing moisture to penetrate to the glueline. This is called face checking. A water-resistant adhesive must be used for plywood exposed to exterior conditions. If surface checks allow water to enter and become trapped, some decay can be expected in unprotected, nondurable wood species. For these species, the first step in finishing should be application of a water-repellent preservative.

Plywood face veneers generally do not exceed 1/4 inch in thickness and are usually about 1/8 inch thick. Therefore, excessive surface erosion, particularly of light-density species such as western redcedar and redwood, can expose the dark-colored glueline within 7 to 10 years (Fig. 22). Consequently, plywood should always be protected with a finish that contains a pigment. The more pigment used, the greater the protection (paints offer greater protection than do stains, particularly latex paints because they are less likely to check). Transparent finishes containing ultraviolet radiation stabilizers and water repellents are generally less effective at protecting the plywood surface and are not recommended.

Hardboard, flakeboard, and particleboard rapidly degrade if they are not protected with a good paint system. In fact, flakeboard and particleboard may deteriorate even with a good paint system. These products often do not have sufficient adhesive to withstand exterior exposure. Cyclic wetting and drying of the board

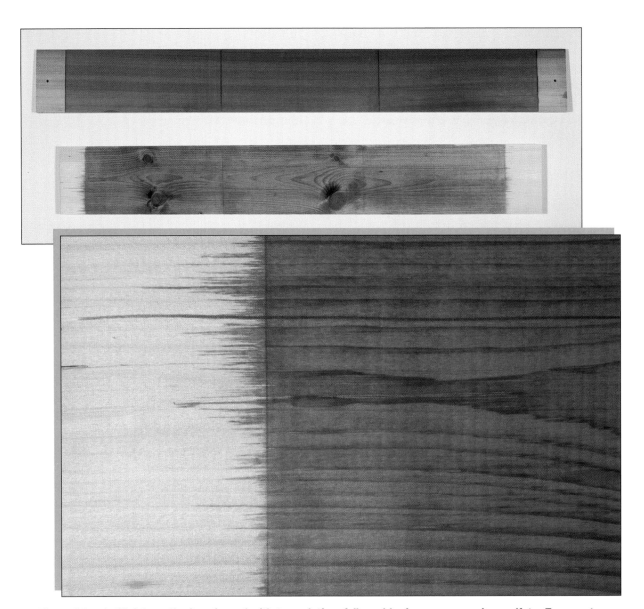

Figure 31.—Artificial weathering of wood with tea solution, followed by ferrous ammonium sulfate. Top, western redcedar and white pine. Bottom, close-up view of untreated (left) and treated (right) parts of white pine board.

places sufficient stress to weaken the adhesive bond of the surface flakes, particles, or fibers. Within several months of weathering, individual flakes, particles, or fiber bundles may separate from the surface. Deeper and deeper layers are subsequently affected at an accelerated rate. Wetting also causes springback of the wood particles, which results from the release of compression set in the particles during the manufacture of the board. Cyclic moisture changes can also cause loss of strength and thickness swelling. If used in exterior exposure, the surfaces of hardboard and particleboard, including the edges, must be coated with high-quality opaque finishes such as paints or solid-color stains.

5

TYPES OF EXTERIOR WOOD FINISHES

The selection of an exterior wood finish depends on the protection needed for the wood (i.e., as determined by its characteristics). Conversely, the amount of protection provided to the wood surface depends on the type of finish. Finished wood is a marriage of two widely different materials, and the properties of both must be considered to achieve the most durable wood/finish system.

Finishes can be divided into two general categories: 1) opaque coatings, such as paints and solid-color stains, and 2) natural finishes, such as water repellents, water-repellent preservatives, oils, and semitransparent penetrating stains. Wood preservatives and fire-retardant coatings might also be called finishes in some respects. The suitability of different finishes and expected service life for various types of exterior wood surfaces are summarized in Table 3. The data were obtained from tests using typical finishes and may not be appropriate for many new formulations. Finish formulations are rapidly being changed to meet clean air legislation. Many finishes traditionally used to coat wood contained volatile organic compounds

(VOCs). Most paint companies are reformulating their finishes to meet current legislative requirements.

Volatile Organic Compounds

Volatile organic compounds are those organic materials in finishes that evaporate as the finish dries and/or cures. These materials are regarded as air pollutants, and the amount that can be released for a given amount of solids (binder, pigments, etc.) in the paints is now regulated in many areas. Legislation in California forced drastic decreases in the VOC content of architectural finish. Similar legislation is in place in areas of New York, Texas, New Jersey, and Arizona; legislation is pending in many other states.

Existing and pending regulations are a serious concern throughout the U.S. paint industry. Nationally, the EPA has been charged under the 1990 New Clean Air Act to enact a regulation that will affect areas of the country that have not previously had to comply with VOC regulations. Previously, manufacturers marketing their products in limited geographic areas outside

Table 3—Suitability and expected service life of finishes for exterior wood surfaces.[a]

Type of exterior wood surface	Water-repellent preservative and oil		Semitransparent stain		Paint and solid-color stain	Paint	Solid-color stain
	Suitability	Expected life[b] (years)	Suitability	Expected life[c] (years)	Suitability	Expected life[d] years	Expected life[d] years
Siding							
Cedar and redwood							
Smooth (vertical grain)	High	1-2	Moderate	2-4	High	4-6	3-5
Roughsawn	High	2-3	High	5-8	High	5-7	4-6
Pine, fir, spruce							
Smooth (flat-grained)	High	1-2	Low	2-3	Moderate	3-5	3-4
Rough (flat-grained)	High	2-3	High	4-7	Moderate	4-6	4-5
Shingles							
Sawn	High	2-3	High	4-8	Moderate	3-5	3-4
Split	High	1-2	High	4-8	–	3-5	3-4
Plywood (Douglas-fir and Southern Pine)							
Sanded	Low	1-2	Moderate	2-4	Moderate	2-4	2-3
Textured (smooth)	Low	1-2	Moderate	2-4	Moderate	3-4	2-3
Textured (roughsawn)	Low	2-3	High	4-8	Moderate	4-6	3-5
Medium-density overlay[e]	–	–	–	–	Excellent	6-8	5-7
Plywood (cedar and redwood)							
Sanded	Low	1-2	Moderate	2-4	Moderate	2-4	2-3
Textured (smooth)	Low	1-2	Moderate	2-4	Moderate	3-4	2-3
Textured (roughsawn)	Low	2-3	High	5-8	Moderate	4-6	3-5
Hardboard, medium density[f]							
Smooth							
Unfinished	–	–	–	–	High	4-6	3-5
Preprimed	–	–	–	–	High	4-6	3-5
Textured							
Unfinished	–	–	–	–	High	4-6	3-5
Preprimed	–	–	–	–	High	4-6	3-5
Millwork (usually pine)							
Windows, shutters, doors, exterior trim	High[g]	–	Moderate	2-3	High	3-6	3-4
Decking							
New (smooth)	High	1-2	Moderate	2-3	Low	2-3	1-2
Weathered (rough)	High	2-3	High	3-6	Low	2-3	1-2
Glued-laminated members							
Smooth	High	1-2	Moderate	3-4	Moderate	3-4	2-3
Rough	High	2-3	High	6-8	Moderate	3-5	3-4
Oriented strandboard	–	–	Low	1-3	Moderate	2-4	2-3

[a] These data were compiled from the observations of many researchers. Expected life predictions are for an average location in the continental United States; expected life will vary in extreme climates or exposure (such as desert, seashore, and deep woods).
[b] Development of mildew on surface indicates need for refinishing.
[c] Smooth, unweathered surfaces are generally finished with only one coat of stain. Roughsawn or weathered surfaces, which are more adsorptive, can be finished with two coats; the second coat is applied while the first coat is still wet.
[d] Expected life of two coats, one primer and one top-coat. Applying a second top-coat (three-coat job) will approximately double the life. Top-quality acrylic latex paints will have the best durability.
[e] Medium-density overlay is generally painted.
[f] Semitransparent stains are not suitable for hardboard. Solid-color stains (acrylic latex) will perform like paints. Paints are preferred.
[g] Exterior millwork, such as windows, should be factory treated according to Industry Standard 1S4-81. Other trim should be liberally treated by brushing before painting.

those affected by existing state and local legislation had been unaffected by VOC regulations. In response to the legislation, all major paint companies have had to either change their paint formulation or market additional low-VOC formulations.

Many traditional wood finishes may no longer be acceptable, including oil-based semitransparent stains, oil- and alkyd-based primers and top coats, solventborne water repellents, and solventborne water-repellent preservatives. Many current wood finishes, including some latex-based materials, may be reformulated. These changes affect the properties of the finish, its application, and its interaction with the wood (e.g., adhesion, penetration, moisture-excluding effectiveness).

There is little information about the degradation mechanisms of these finishes when exposed to various outdoor conditions. Since these new formulations may not interact with the wood in the same way as do traditional finishes, they may have a different effect on moisture absorption.

Effect of Finishes on Moisture Absorption

The various dimensions of wood and wood-based building materials are constantly changing because of changes in moisture content, which in turn are caused by fluctuations in the atmospheric relative humidity as well as rain or dew. Water repellents provide protection against liquid water but are ineffective against water vapor (humidity). Film-forming finishes such as paint and varnish shed liquid water and retard the absorption of water vapor, provided the films are thick enough. Because film-forming wood finishes like paint will last longer on stable wood, it is desirable to stabilize the wood by finishing it with a water-repellent preservative as the first step in the finish system.

The protection of wood from moisture through applying a finish or coating depends on many variables. Among the variables are thickness of the coating film, absence of defects and voids in the film, type of pigment (if any), chemical composition of the vehicle or resin, volume ratio of pigment to vehicle, vapor pressure gradient across the film, and length of exposure period. Regardless of the number of coatings used, the coating can never be entirely moisture-proof. In the absence of wetting by liquid water, the moisture content of the wood depends on the ambient relative humidity. The coating simply slows down the rate at which the wood changes moisture content.

Film-forming finishes slow both the absorption of water vapor and drying of the wood.

Figure 32 shows the effect of three coats of highly effective alkyd paint on the moisture content of ponderosa pine sapwood. This laboratory formulation was about 80 percent effective at blocking water vapor absorption compared with water absorption of an unpainted control. In addition, the paint slowed the rate of drying. In cyclic high and low relative humidities, the moisture content of the wood increased with time (Fig. 33). This retardation of drying can have a drastic effect on the durability of painted wood fully exposed to the weather. The moisture content of the wood can approach the range where decay fungi can become active. All common film-forming finishes, both oil and latex, show the same absorption and desorption characteristics as this laboratory formulation, but to a lesser extent.

In addition to absorbing and desorbing water vapor, paint coatings usually crack at the joint between two pieces of wood, particularly if they have different grain orientations (i.e., different dimensional stability). Water enters the wood through these cracks and is trapped by the coating (Figs. 34, 38, and 43). The wood moisture content can quickly reach the range at which decay fungi can flourish. Pretreatment with water-repellent preservatives can retard water absorption if the paint film cracks.

The degree of protection provided by different treatments depends on the type of exposure. For example, water-repellent treatments are ineffective against exposure to water vapor, but relatively effective against free water for a short exposure time. The absorption and desorption of water vapor to and from wood treated with a water-repellent preservative is similar to the curve shown for unfinished wood in Figures 32 and 33. To achieve good moisture-excluding effectiveness (slow water vapor absorption), a build-up of a film-forming finish (two and preferably three coats) is required because mere plugging of the wood pores is not effective. The cell walls at the surface must likewise be fully covered. The first or primer coat applied to bare wood is rarely effective at slowing water vapor absorption. Thus, backpriming of siding allows the wood to breathe, yet blocks the bleeding of extractives. Water-repellent preservatives are especially effective for treating the back side of siding.

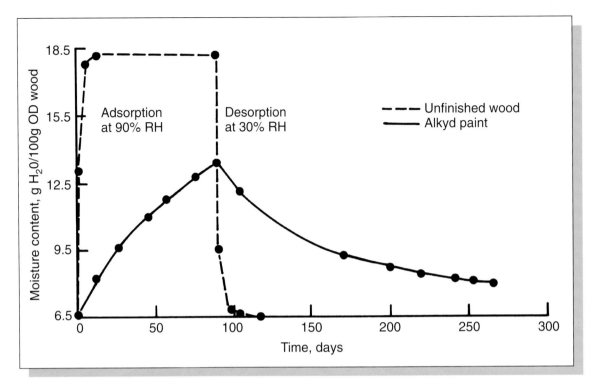

Figure 32.—Change in moisture content of ponderosa pine sapwood finished with three coats of aluminum pigmented alkyd paint and exposed to 90 and 30 percent relative humidity at 80°F, compared to unfinished wood.

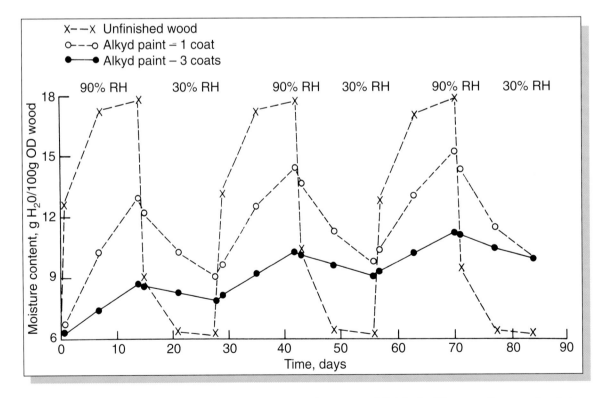

Figure 33.—Change in moisture content of ponderosa pine sapwood finished with one or three coats of aluminum pigmented alkyd paint and exposed to alternating cycles of 90 and 30 percent relative humidity at 80°F, compared to unfinished wood.

For a coating to be effective at minimizing moisture content changes of the wood, it must be applied to all wood surfaces, **particularly the end grain**. The end grain of wood absorbs moisture much faster than does the face grain, and finishes generally fail in this area first (Fig. 34). In those houses where moisture is moving from the living quarters to the outside wall because there is either no vapor retarder or a poor one, the application of moisture-excluding finishes to the outside will not prevent paint peeling.

Opaque Finishes

Paint

Paints provide the most protection to wood against surface erosion by weathering and against wetting by water (Fig. 35). They conceal some surface defects and provide color. Pigments increase paint opacity and eliminate ultraviolet radiation degradation of the wood surface. Oil-based or alkyd-based paints are a suspension of inorganic pigments in an oil or chemically modified oil and turpentine or mineral spirit solvent. The oils are often referred to as resins, vehicles, or binders, and the solvent helps carry the pigment particles and the resin to the wood surface. The oils cure by reacting with oxygen in the air to form a cross-linked polymeric film. The more highly cross-linked the polymer, the more resistant the polymer to water (both vapor and liquid). Latex paints are likewise a suspension of inorganic pigments and various latex resins, but the solvent or dispersant in this case is mostly water. Latex paints form a film by the coalescence of small spheres of polymers dispersed in water. The polymers are more flexible and not as highly cross-linked as cured oil-based paints, and therefore they provide less barrier to moisture.

Note: Although paint can prevent moisture from entering wood, paint is not a preservative. It will not prevent decay if conditions are favorable for fungal growth.

Although oil-based paint films usually provide the best shield against liquid water, water vapor, and discoloration by wood extractives, they become brittle over time. On the other hand, latex paints, particularly all-acrylic paint,

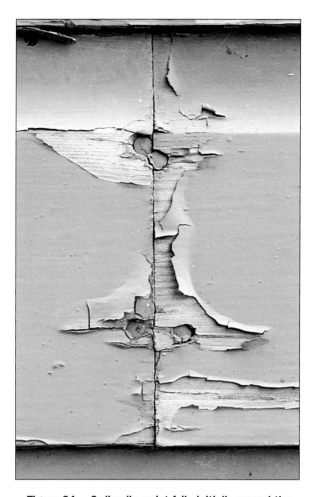

Figure 34.—Ordinarily, paint fails initially around the ends and edges of a board. Liberal application of a water repellent or water-repellent preservative, especially to the end grain, can prolong the service life of paint in these areas.

remain more flexible with age. Even though latex paints are more porous to both liquid water and water vapor, they are better able to accommodate dimensional changes in the wood by stretching and shrinking with the wood. However, unless specially formulated to block extractives bleed, latex paint films are prone to show this type of discoloration. Research at the Forest Products Laboratory, in Madison, Wisconsin, and other laboratories showed that all-acrylic latex top-coat paints, applied in two coats over a stain-blocking acrylic latex primer, last longer than other paint systems, even on difficult-to-paint surfaces. Latex paints are easier to use than oil-based paints because water is used for cleanup.

Figure 35.—Two structures maintained with good painting practices. (Photos courtesy of Southern Forest Productions Association.)

Paints perform best on edge-grained lumber of light-density species such as redwood and cedar. If used on flat-grained lumber, a rough-sawn surface improves the service life. Although the binder in primers may absorb superficially into the tangential and radial surfaces, for all practical purposes paints remain primarily on

the wood surface to form a film. The wood grain is completely obscured by the surface film.

The cost of finishes varies widely depending on the type of finish and quality (Table 4). Within a particular type of finish (e.g., oil-based paint, all-acrylic latex paint, oil-based solid-color stain, etc.), the cost usually correlates with

Table 4—Initial application and maintenance of exterior wood finishes.[a]

Finish	Initial application		Appearance of wood	Maintenance		
	Process	Cost		Process	Cost	Timing
Water-repellent preservative	Brushing	Low	Grain visible; wood brown to black, fades slightly with age	Brush to remove surface dirt	Low	1-3 years
	Pressure (factory applied)	Medium	Grain visible; wood greenish or brownish, fades with age	Brush to remove surface dirt	Nil, unless stained, painted, or varnished	None, unless stained, painted, or varnished
Organic solvent preservative[b]	Pressure, steeping, dipping, and brushing	Low to medium	Grain visible; color as desired	Brush and reapply	Medium	2-3 years or when preferred
Water repellent and oils[c]	One or two brush coats of clear material or, preferably, dip application	Low	Grain and natural color visible, becoming darker and rougher textured with age	Clean and reapply	Low to medium	1-3 years or when preferred
Semitransparent stain	One or two brush coats	Low to medium	Grain visible; color as desired	Clean and reapply	Low to medium	3-6 years or when preferred
Clear varnish	Three coats (minimum)	High	Grain and natural color unchanged if adequately maintained	Clean, sand, and stain bleached areas; apply two more coats	High	2 years or when break down begins[d]
Paint and solid-color stain	Brushing: water repellent, prime, and two top coats	Medium to high	Grain and natural color obscured	Clean and apply top coat, or remove and repeat initial treatment if damaged	Medium	7-10 years for paint[e]; 3-7 years for solid-color stain

[a] This table is a compilation of data from the observations of many researchers.
[b] Pentachlorophenol, bis(tri-n-butyltin oxide), copper naphthenate, copper-8-quinolinolate, and similar materials.
[c] With or without added preservatives. Addition of preservative helps control mildew growth.
[d] Application of a semitransparent stain prior to varnishing extends the service life of the varnish.
[e] If top-quality acrylic latex top-coats are used.

quality. Better quality paints usually contain higher amounts of solids by weight. Paints with a lower percentage of solids may cost less by the gallon but be more expensive per pound of solids and more or heavier coats will have to be applied to achieve equal coverage. A comparison of the ratio of solids content to price can be the first criterion for selecting the better value because only the solids remain on the wood surface after the solvent evaporates. For example, a 50-percent solids paint that costs $20/gal is a better value than a 40-percent solids paint that costs $18/gal. Another criterion is the amount and type of pigment, which determines the hiding power of the finish. A paint with poor hiding power may require more coats. Finally, the type and amount of binder affects the quality of the paint. For latex paints, all-acrylic binders are more weather-resistant than vinyl and vinyl-acrylic binders.

Research at the Forest Products Laboratory does not include consumer testing of paints or other finishes. Finishes are evaluated by generic type only and with regard to how they perform on a specific substrate. For example, a study may focus on the difference in performance between a waterborne and solventborne paint on roughsawn Douglas-fir.

Solid-Color Stains

Solid-color stains (also called heavy-bodied or opaque stains) are opaque finishes that come in a wide range of colors and are essentially paints. Like paints, solid-color stains protect wood against degradation by ultraviolet radiation. Solid-color stains are made with a much higher concentration of pigment than are semitransparent penetrating stains, but with a somewhat lower concentration of pigment than standard paints. As a result, solid-color stains obscure the natural wood color and grain; some surface texture is retained and the finish appears flat. Like paints, solid-color stains form a film and can cover old films. They can also blister, flake, and peel like paints. Solid-color stains are not penetrating finishes as are solventborne oil-based semitransparent stains. They should not be applied over wood previously finished with penetrating finishes (water-repellent preservatives or oil-based semitransparent stains), without special surface preparation. The weathered surface must be sanded to assure adhesion of the film.

Solid-color stains are available in both latex-based and oil-based formulations. The acrylic-latex-based versions are generally the best choice because they have superior resistance to sunlight. Oil-based formulations have the advantage of requiring a lower minimum temperature for curing. Solid-color stains are often used on textured surfaces and panel products such as hardboard and plywood. These stains are most effective when applied in two or three coats, especially as two top coats over a quality primer. Oil-based solid-color stains applied as a single coat on flat-grained wood are prone to flake.

Natural Finishes

In many locations throughout the United States, there is a continuing trend toward the use of natural colors and finishes to protect exterior wood siding and trim. Architects, builders, and owners are specifying a "natural look" for homes, apartments, churches, and commercial buildings. To some, a natural look means rough, gray, and weathered (Fig. 30). To others, a successful natural exterior wood finish is one that retains the original, attractive appearance of the wood with the least change in color and the least masking of wood grain and surface texture (Fig. 36). In this case, the finish should inhibit the growth of mildew microorganisms, protect against moisture and sunlight, and not change the surface appearance or color of the wood.

The most natural appearance for wood is achieved without a protective finish. However, in the normal weathering process, the appearance of unprotected wood exposed outdoors is soon changed by the adverse effects of light,

Figure 36.—House finished with a natural water-repellent preservative.

Table 5—Composition of typical water repellents and water-repellent preservatives.

Ingredient	Approximate composition (percent by weight)	
	Water repellent	Water-repellent preservative
Preservative	0	0.25–5
Resin or drying oil	10	10
Paraffin wax	0.5-1	0.5–1
Solvent (turpentine, mineral spirits, or paint thinner)	89	84–89

moisture, and the growth of micro-organisms on the surface. As described in Chapter 4, Weathering of Wood, the original surface becomes rough as the grain raises and the wood checks. In many humid locations, weathering is often accompanied by a surface growth of dark gray, black, or blotchy mildew that may remain uneven and unsightly until the wood has weathered for many years.

Natural finishes can be divided into two categories: 1) penetrating types, such as transparent water repellents, water-repellent preservatives, oils, and semitransparent oil-based stains, and 2) film-forming types, such as varnishes. Shellacs and lacquers, which are film-forming finishes, are not recommended for exterior use because they are easily damaged by moisture.

Water-Repellent Preservatives

A water-repellent preservative may be used as a natural finish (Fig. 36). This type of finish contains a preservative (a fungicide), a small amount of wax (or similar hydrocarbon as a water repellent), a resin or drying oil, and a solvent such as turpentine, mineral spirits, or paraffinic oil (Table 5). Waterborne formulations are also available. Some water-repellent preservatives contain stabilizers to help decrease degradation by ultraviolet radiation. The wax decreases the absorption of liquid water by the wood (Fig. 37). The preservative prevents wood from darkening (graying) by inhibiting the growth of mildew, and it helps deter decay in aboveground use, particularly when absorbed into the end grain of boards and between joints. Examples of commercial preservatives and their typical concentrations when used in water-repellent preservatives (by weight) are 3-iodo-2-propynyl butyl carbamate, 0.5 percent; copper naphthenate, 2 percent as copper metal; zinc naphthenate, 2 percent as zinc metal; bis(tri-N-butyltin) oxide, 0.15 to 0.675

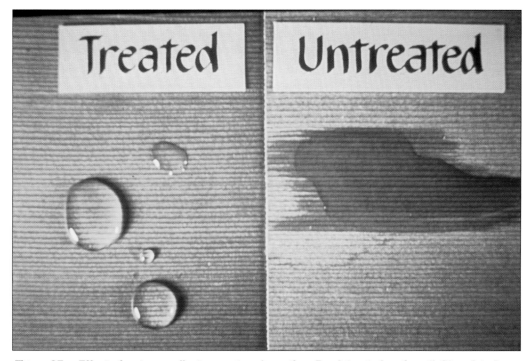

Figure 37.—Effect of water-repellent on water absorption. Brush-treated surface (left) resisted penetration by liquid water, whereas untreated surface (right) absorbed water quickly.

percent; copper-8-quinolinolate, 0.15 to 0.675 percent; N-(trichloromethylthio) phthalmide, 0.5 percent; and 2-(thiocyanomethylthio) benzo thiazole (TCMTB), 0.5 percent.

Water-repellent preservatives are not intended for wood used in ground contact and should not be confused with the preservatives used for pressure treating wood. Water-repellent preservatives give short-term, aboveground protection against decay for untreated wood, sections of pressure-treated wood that are not affected by preservative treatment (heartwood), and the interior of large cross-sections exposed by cutting or drilling. The treatment decreases warping and checking, prevents water staining, and helps control mildew growth. Water-repellent preservatives slow weathering by decreasing the effects of water and give some protection from ultraviolet radiation. However, water-repellent preservatives do not provide as good protection against ultraviolet radiation as do pigmented finishes. Ultraviolet radiation slowly degrades the wood surface. The resulting finish varies in color, depending upon the wood color itself, but usually weathers to a golden tan. If the wood is not refinished, the color will fade to light tan and eventually to light gray.

The initial application of a water-repellent preservative lasts only 1 to 2 years on smooth surfaces and 1 to 3 years on roughsawn or weathered surfaces. When a surface starts to show a blotchy discoloration resulting from extractive bleed or mildew, it should be cleaned with a commercial cleaner or a solution of liquid household bleach and detergent, rinsed well, and retreated after drying (see Mildew, Prevention and Removal in Chapter 9). During the first few years, the finish may have to be applied every year or so. After the wood has gradually weathered to a uniform tan color, additional treatments may last 2 to 4 years because the weathered boards absorb more finish. This type of natural finish is most successful on single-story structures protected from sunlight with large roof overhangs and/or shaded by trees.

Water-repellent preservatives do not normally contain pigments but may darken the wood slightly. They make the wood appear wet. Relatively small quantities of dyes (tinting colors) can be added to the water-repellent preservative solution to match the natural color of the wood. These dyes do not have the durability of pigments, but may give some added protection against ultraviolet radiation.

Some manufacturers market "paintable" water-repellent preservatives. These preservatives contain less wax than other preservatives of this type and can be used as a pretreatment prior to painting new wood or for areas where paint has peeled. This treatment keeps rain or dew from penetrating the wood, especially the end grain, thus decreasing the shrinking and swelling of the wood. As a result, less stress is placed on the paint film, and its service life is extended (Figs. 34 and 38). When the entire board is treated, the wax also decreases the capillary movement of water up the back side of lap or drop siding. The fungicide inhibits decay, mold, and mildew growth. Make certain that the manufacturer's label indicates that the water-repellent preservative is paintable. Some products have too much wax or other water repellents and the paint will not adhere adequately. When spot-treating bare areas on painted wood, take care to avoid getting the water-repellent preservative on the painted area surrounding the bare area. The wax in the water-repellent preservative will not absorb into the paint, and the new paint will peel.

Water repellents are also available. They differ from water-repellent preservatives in the lack of preservative or inclusion of a mildewcide (Table 5). Water-repellent preservatives provide better protection than water repellents, especially in areas with warm wet climates, such as the southern United States.

When using water repellents or water-repellent preservatives, carefully read and follow the manufacturer's specifications. Any type of water-repellent preservative can be used as a natural exterior finish by itself, but only some are paintable. Manufacturers have also developed water-repellent preservatives specifically for exterior natural finishes. In areas where decay is a serious problem or where wood will be in contact with the ground or water, water repellents and water-repellent preservatives do not provide adequate protection. Wood that has

Figure 38.—Effect of water-repellent preservative on paint durability. Top, window sash and frame treated and then painted. Bottom, window sash and frame not treated before painting. In both cases, the window was exposed for 5 years. Note good condition of wood and glazing on treated window.

been pressure treated with an appropriate preservative should be used.

Oils

Many oil or oil-based natural wood finishes are available for finishing exterior wood. The most common drying oils are linseed and tung. However, natural oils are a food source for mildew and may encourage their growth, if used without a mildewcide. Oils protect wood, but their average lifetime may be only as long as that described for water-repellent preservatives.

Semitransparent Penetrating Stains

The Forest Products Laboratory was a fore-runner in the development of a semitransparent stain during the 1950s.[4] Since then, semitransparent penetrating stains have grown in popularity (Fig. 39). These stains are similar to water repellents or water-repellent preservatives, but are pigmented. They penetrate the wood surface, are porous, and do not form a surface film or totally hide the wood grain like paint. By allowing the wood to breathe, stains do not trap moisture that may encourage decay. Because they do not trap moisture, they are conducive to use in high-moisture environments, such as for fences, decks, or structures housing livestock. Stains will not blister or peel even if moisture penetrates the wood.

Penetrating stains have traditionally been oil- or alkyd-based and usually contain a fungicide, ultraviolet radiation stabilizer, and water repellent. The manufacturer's label usually indicates whether the finish resists mildew and often lists a specific mildewcide. Latex-based (waterborne) stains are also available, but they do not penetrate the wood surface as well as their oil-based counterparts. New latex formulations being developed may provide better penetrating characteristics.

Pigments determine the appearance, opacity, and durability of stains. The more pigment in a stain, the better its durability, the deeper its color, and the more it hides the color and figure of the wood. Consequently, the less transparent the finish, the less natural the wood appears.

Semitransparent penetrating stains are most effective on roughsawn and weathered wood because more finish can be applied. They can be used on flat-grained surfaces of dense species, such as southern pine, that do not hold paint well. They also provide satisfactory performance on smooth lumber surfaces, but not smooth

---

[4]Black, John M., Don F. Laughnan, and Edward A. Mraz. Forest Products Laboratory Natural Finish. Research Note FPL-046. Madison, WI: U.S. Department of Agriculture, Forest Service, Forest Products Laboratory. Rev. 1975. 8 p.

Figure 39.—Modern house finished with penetrating oil-based stains. (Photo courtesy of Southern Forest Products Association.)

plywood surfaces. Available from commercial sources in a variety of colors, semitransparent penetrating stains are especially popular in brown or red earth tones, which provide a natural or rustic appearance to the wood.

If used on new smooth-planed siding fully exposed to the weather, semitransparent penetrating stain generally lasts about 2 to 4 years (Table 3). Generally, smooth wood accepts only a single coat. If a second coat is applied, it may form a film instead of penetrating the wood. This causes the stain to appear shiny, and the film may flake from the surface as it weathers. When refinished after weathering, the finish will usually last much longer, and the surface should accept two coats of stain. Two coats of stain applied to roughsawn or weathered surfaces may last 6 to 8 years or more. In general, oil- or alkyd-based semitransparent stains provide at least two to three times the service life of unpigmented water-repellent preservatives.

When finishing the smooth-planed siding of high-density species such as southern pine and Douglas-fir, the surface may be treated with a water-repellent preservative and allowed to weather for a year before staining. The first coat of stain will then penetrate uniformly and be more durable because weathering has made the wood surface more absorptive.

Semitransparent penetrating stains can only be used over other penetrating finishes, such as oils or water-repellent preservatives. Even over penetrating finishes, stains will not penetrate the wood unless the surface has weathered. If the finish penetrates well into the previously finished surface, it will appear flat. If the finish does not penetrate, it will dry slowly with many glossy areas. Semitransparent stains must not be applied over film-forming finishes such as varnish, paint, and solid-color stain. Even if these films are removed from the wood, absorption of the stain may be hampered by residual coating on the wood.

> **NOTE:** Semitransparent stains are not recommended for hardboard, waferboard, oriented strandboard, and similar wood composites.

Transparent Film-Forming Finishes

Transparent film-forming finishes, such as spar, urethane, and marine varnishes, are not generally recommended for exterior use on wood. Ultraviolet radiation penetrates the transparent film and degrades the wood. Regardless of the number of coats, the finish will eventually become brittle as a result of exposure to sunlight, develop severe cracks, and peel, often in less than 2 years (Fig. 40). Photochemically degraded fibers peel from the wood along with the finish. Clear coatings can be used in a few special circumstances, such as exterior doors that are protected by a porch, lawn furniture that is protected when not in use, and soffits. Note that even areas that are well-protected from sunlight and water require a minimum of three coats of finish, and the wood should be treated initially with a paintable water-repellent preservative. The use of varnish-compatible pigmented stains and sealers as an undercoat will also contribute to a longer life of clear finishes. For marine exposures, six coats of varnish should be applied for best performance.

Finely ground iron oxide, titanium dioxide, and/or other pigments which are transparent to visible light, are being used in a number of clear film-forming finishes. These transparent pigments act much like an opaque pigment and give some protection to the wood, thereby improving the durability of the coating. Varnish containing transparent iron oxide is less likely to fail by debonding from the wood. The transparent pigments significantly improve the service life of the varnish, but the finish still undergoes surface deterioration.

A finish that partially penetrates the wood and forms a film has been developed in Europe. This finish is commonly called a varnish stain. Varnish stain forms a surface layer that is thicker than a semitransparent stain but thinner than varnish. Varnish stains contain a water repellent, transparent iron oxide pigments, and a mildewcide. The surface coating slowly erodes and can be refinished more easily than a conventional varnish.

There are two other types of film-forming transparent finishes, but neither works well in exterior applications. Two-part polyurethanes or epoxies are tougher and perhaps more

Figure 40.—Transparent finishes like varnish generally crack and peel in less than 2 years unless protected from sun and rain.

resistant to ultraviolet radiation than other transparent film-forming coatings, but they are expensive, are difficult to use, and usually have as short a life as conventional varnishes. The second type, lacquer and shellac, is **not** suitable for exterior application, even as a sealer or primer, because these finishes have little resistance to moisture. In addition, they are usually brittle and thus crack and check easily. However, pigmented knot sealers based on shellac are available for exterior application. These knot sealers must be protected with a finish and should be used on knots only.

Fire-Retardant Finishes

Some finishes may slightly decrease the flammability of wood products when applied in a conventional thickness, but most finishes will burn. The finish provides additional fuel in a fire, particularly if the film is a build-up of many layers of paint. Commercial fire-retardant, paint-like finishes have been developed that provide varying degrees of protection against fire. Fire-retardant finishes generally have low surface flammability characteristics. The finishes form an expanded low-density film upon exposure to fire (intumesce), thus insulating the wood surface from heat and retarding burning. Additional ingredients restrict the flaming of any released combustible vapors. These finishes may also contain chemicals that promote decomposition of the wood to charcoal and water rather than to the formation of volatile flammable products.

Most fire-retardant finishes are intended for interior use, although leach-resistant fire-retardants have been developed for exterior use. These chemicals are usually diffused into the wood under pressure much like wood preservatives. Conventional paints can be applied over fire-retardant-treated wood to help prevent weathering and/or leaching of the fire retardant.

APPLICATION OF EXTERIOR WOOD FINISHES

How a finish is applied to wood is as important for durability and good performance as what finish/substrate combination is selected for the job. Finishes can be brushed, rolled, sprayed, or applied by dipping. The application technique used, the quantity of finish applied, the surface condition of the substrate, and the weather conditions at the time of application can substantially affect the life expectancy of the finish. The following section includes application methods for both film-forming and penetrating finishes. For optimum performance, these application guidelines should be used in concert with the manufacturer's directions for the product.

Conditions that Affect the Finish

Weathering

Because weathering is a surface deterioration, the amount of weathering that new wood undergoes prior to finishing has a direct affect on the type of finish that can be used, the application rate, and the performance of the finish. The eroded and roughened surface of weathered wood can prevent proper adhesion of a film-forming finish; exposure of wood for only a few weeks is sufficient to cause this loss of adhesion. On the other hand, weathering of smooth planed wood can enhance the performance of oil-based semitransparent stains.

Wood finishes also undergo photochemical degradation, but the mode of degradation is different for penetrating finishes (stains and water repellents) than for film-forming finishes (paints). Photochemical degradation is addressed in Chapter 4, Weathering of Wood.

Preservative Treatment

Finish characteristics of preservative-treated wood are primarily dependent on wood species and grain orientation (flat- or vertical-grained) of the lumber. Preservative-treated lumber is not graded according to grain orientation. Therefore, species like southern pine generally contain wide bands of latewood, which can create finishing problems. Stain penetration is poor on such latewood bands and early finish failure is likely, particularly in structures fully exposed to the weather.

Waterborne preservative treatments **do not** adversely affect the finishing characteristics of wood. In fact, treatment with chromated copper arsenate (CCA) actually enhances the durability of finishes, particularly semitransparent stains. The chromium oxides in CCA, which bond to the wood after treatment, decrease photodegradation of the wood surface and can increase the durability of semitransparent stains two to three times. Note that ammoniacal copper zinc arsenate (ACZA) and copper oxide/quaternary ammonium compounds (ACQ) do not contain chromium oxides, and therefore the performance of stains on the treated lumber will be similar to that of untreated wood, given similar finish coverage and exposure conditions.

Other preservative pressure treatments for wood, including pentachlorophenol (penta) in light or heavy oils and creosote, are intended for retaining walls, railroad cross-ties, and other heavy industrial uses. They should not be used on wood decks or other areas that come in contact with humans or animals. Penta in heavy oil and creosote will not hold paint, and lumber treated with these materials does not absorb semitransparent stains well. Wood treated with penta in light oil or solvent can be finished with a penetrating finish after 1 or 2 years of weathering.

Moisture Content

The main consideration in finishing pressure-treated lumber is the moisture content of the wood. In some cases, the lumber may still be wet from the pressure treatment when it is delivered to the job site, particularly during cool or wet weather. If the wood is still wet, it must be allowed to dry before finishing so that the surface moisture content is less than 20 percent. The rate wood dries once in place in a completed structure depends on weather conditions; under warm summer conditions, about 2 to 3 weeks should be sufficient for drying. For best finish performance, the wood should be at a moisture content typical of what it will be during service-life—about 12 percent moisture content for most areas of the continental United States. Moisture content will vary as the climate changes, and it will seldom be consistent throughout a board.

Opaque Finishes

Paint

Wood and wood-based products should be protected from the weather before, during, and after construction. For new construction, it is seldom necessary to give wood extensive surface preparation if it is clean and dry. Surface contamination from dirt, oil, and other foreign substances must be eliminated. All paints and primers should contain a mildewcide. The performance of the mildewcide in the paint can be enhanced by pretreatment of the wood with a water-repellent preservative (for details see subsection on Water-Repellent Preservatives in Chapter 5). Weather permitting, wood should be painted as soon as possible after installation. Research has shown that even a 3- to 4-week exposure of a freshly planed wood surface to the weather (especially the sun) can adversely affect the adhesion of paint to the wood. Wood that has weathered badly before painting will have a degraded surface that is not good for painting, and paint will be more likely to peel from such wood. If it is necessary to paint weathered wood, such as to refinish a painted area that has peeled, the weathered wood should be sanded and washed before painting.

Some surface preparation may be necessary under some circumstances, even with new wood. Smooth-planed, flat-grained surfaces may not hold paint very well. The surface may have crushed grain and be slightly burnished from planing. For flat-grained lumber, wet the surface thoroughly, let it dry for a day or two, and scuff-sand the surface with rough sandpaper (50 to 80 grit). Wetting will relieve crushed grain at the surface and sanding will greatly increase paint adhesion (Fig. 10). This procedure is unnecessary for roughsawn lumber, even if it is flat-grained.

To achieve maximum paint life, follow these steps:

1. Treat the wood with a paintable water-repellent preservative. Warm weather is preferred to assure proper penetration of the water repellent. Lap and butt joints and the edges of panel products such as plywood, hardboard, and particleboard should be well treated since paint normally fails in these areas first (Fig. 34). Allow at least 3 warm, sunny days for adequate drying before priming, caulking joints, and top coating the treated surface. If the wood is painted before the solvent from the water-repellent preservative can evaporate, the paint applied over the treated wood may be slow to dry, may discolor, or may dry with a rough surface that resembles alligator hide. If the wood has been dip treated, allow it to dry for at least 1 week of warm weather. The small amount of wax (less than 1 percent) in a paintable water-repellent preservative will not prevent proper adhesion of the paint if the water-repellent preservative is allowed to cure sufficiently after treatment.

2. Prime the wood as soon as possible after the water-repellent preservative has cured. The primer coat is very important because it forms a base for all succeeding paint coats. For woods with water-soluble extractives, such as redwood and western redcedar, the primer must seal in or tie up the extractives so that they will not bleed through the top coat. Use a good-quality oil-based, alkyd-based, or stain-blocking acrylic latex-based primer; the label should clearly state that the primer can block extractives bleed. The primer should also be nonporous and thus inhibit the penetration of rain or dew into the wood surfaces, which decreases the tendency of the wood to shrink and swell. A primer should be used whether the top coat is an oil-based or latex-based paint. For species such as pine or others that are predominately sapwood and relatively free of extractives compared with redwood, a high-quality acrylic latex primer is preferred. The primer should not be spread too thin; it should obscure the wood grain. The application rates recommended by the manufacturer should be followed. A primer coat that is uniform, flexible, and of the proper thickness will distribute the swelling stresses that develop in wood and thus prevent premature paint failure. The top coat should be applied as soon as the primer coat is dry—about 48 hours for oil-based paints—or as recommended by the manufacturer. Special primers are available for knots.

3. Apply two coats of a good-quality, all-acrylic latex house paint over the primer. If it is not practical to apply two top-coats to the entire house, two top-coats must be applied to fully exposed areas on the south and west sides to obtain good protection. Areas fully exposed to sun and rain are the first to deteriorate. Vinyl-acrylic, modified-acrylic, and oil-based top-coat paints can also be used; however, the all-acrylic formulations have the best resistance to sunlight. Allow the first coat of oil-based paint to cure for 1 to 2 days before applying the second coat. In cold or damp weather, an extra day or two should be allowed between coat applications. Coats of latex paint can usually be applied within a few hours of each other. On those wood surfaces best suited for painting, one coat of a good house paint (acrylic latex) over a properly applied primer (a conventional two-coat paint system) should last 4 to 5 years, but two top-coats over one primer coat can last up to 10 years.

Apply 1 gallon of paint per approximately 400 ft.² of smooth or scuff-sanded wood surface area. For roughsawn wood, the coverage will be considerably less than 400 ft.²/gal. However, coverage can vary with different paints, surface characteristics, and application procedures. Research has indicated that the optimum thickness for the total dry paint coat (primer and two top-coats) is 3.5 to 5 mil or about the thickness of a sheet of newspaper. Some paints (especially latex) will successfully cover the primer coat at one-half this thickness, but these thin coats will erode rapidly. On the other hand, thick paint coats tend to build up and develop cracks. The coverage of a paint coat should be checked occasionally by measuring the area covered for a set volume of paint used to ensure that the coverage corresponds to that recommended by the manufacturer. Brush application is superior to roller, spray, or painting-pad application, especially for the first coat. Professional painters can usually spray paint and obtain good performance. If the paint is applied by spray or roller, back brushing helps work the finish into the wood and even out the coating, particularly on rough surfaces. Back brushing primer paint increases the service life of the paint system.

To avoid future debonding between paint coats, the first top-coat should be applied within 2 weeks of the primer and the second top-coat within 2 weeks of the first. As certain primer paints weather, they can form a soap-like substance on their surface that may prevent proper adhesion of new paint coats. If more than 2 weeks elapse before applying another paint coat, scrub the old surface with water using a bristle brush or sponge. If necessary, use a mild detergent to remove all dirt and deteriorated paint; if mildew develops, clean the surface with a commercial cleaner or bleach (see Mildew, Prevention and Removal in Chapter 9). Then, rinse the surface with water and allow it to dry before painting. If the primer has weathered for more than 2 weeks, check for good top coat adhesion in a small area before painting the entire structure.

To avoid temperature blisters, oil-based paints should not be applied on a cool surface that will be heated by the sun within a few hours. When painting, follow the sun around the structure. Temperature blisters are most common on thick coats of dark paint applied in cool weather. The blisters usually appear in the last coat of paint and occur within a few hours to 1 or 2 days after painting. Unlike blisters caused by moisture, they do not contain water.

Oil-based paint may be applied when the temperature is 40°F or above. A minimum of 50°F is desirable for applying latex-based paints. For proper curing of latex paint films, the temperature should not drop below 50°F for at least 24 hours after paint application. Low temperatures will result in poor coalescence of the paint film and early paint failure.

Wrinkling, fading, or loss of gloss of oil-based paints and streaking of latex paints can be avoided by not applying paint in the evening, when heavy dew can form before the surface of the paint has thoroughly dried. Serious water absorption problems and major finish failure can also occur with some latex paints when applied under these conditions. Allow at least 2 hours drying time before sunset. Likewise, do not begin painting in the morning until the dew has evaporated.

Solid-Color Stains

Solid-color stains may be applied to wood by brush, roller, or pad, but brush application is usually the best. These stains act much like paint. They are not generally recommended for

---

Paint adhesion to smooth wood can be improved by scratch-sanding the smooth surface with 50 to 80 grit sandpaper prior to priming. This roughening will improve adhesion but will not detract from a smooth high-gloss finish, after top coating.

Power washing, particularly with a sand-water mixture, can change surface texture. If done carefully and at low pressure, power washing increases roughness, thus improving adhesion, and has the added benefit of relaxing surface stresses in the wood. If the pressure is too high and/or the nozzle is held too close to the wood surface, power washing can erode too much wood, leaving the surface less able to hold paint properly.

horizontal wood surfaces such as deck boards, railings, and window sills. One coat of solid-color stain is only marginally adequate on new wood. Two coats will always provide better protection and longer service. The best performance can be obtained if the wood is primed, then given two coats of stain. The all-acrylic, latex solid-color stains are generally superior to all others, especially when two coats are applied over a primer. Oil-based solid-color stains are often used on staining-type woods such as cedar and redwood. As with paints, oil-based solid-color stains can be applied at lower temperatures than can latex solid-color stains.

Unlike paint, a solid-color stain may leave lap marks. Latex-based stains are fast-drying and are more likely to show lap marks than are oil-based stains. To prevent lap marks, follow the procedures suggested under application of semitransparent penetrating stains.

Natural Finishes

Water-Repellent Preservatives

Water-repellent preservatives should only be used on bare wood or on wood previously treated with this kind of preservative. For new construction, the most effective method of applying a water-repellent preservative is to dip the entire board into the solution. However, brush, roller, and pad application is also effective. When wood is treated after the structure has been completed, liberal amounts of the solution should be applied to all lap and butt joints, edges and ends of boards, and edges of panels having end grain. Other areas especially vulnerable to moisture, such as the bottom of doors and window frames, need to be treated. One gallon of preservative will cover about 250 ft.^{2} of smooth surface or 100 to 150 ft.^{2} of rough surface. When used as a natural finish, the service life of a water-repellent preservative on new wood is only 1 to 2 years, depending upon the wood and exposure (Table 4). Treatments on rough and/or weathered surfaces generally last longer than those on smooth surfaces. Dip treatment of lumber prior to installation or repeated brush treatment to the point of refusal will enhance the finish durability. The more finish absorbed by the wood, the longer the service life. **If a water-repellent preservative is used as a pretreatment before painting, apply only during warm weather, apply only a single coat, and use caution to avoid excessive build-up of wax on the surface.**

Weathered wood is conducive to finishing with any penetrating finish, including water-repellent preservatives and semitransparent penetrating stains. Weathering opens up checks and cracks, thus allowing the wood to absorb and retain more preservative or stain, so the finish is generally more durable. However, weathered wood requires much more finish than does unweathered wood.

CAUTION: Water repellents and water-repellent preservatives should always be mixed, handled, and applied carefully. The safest place for mixing is outdoors. Solutions with solvents are volatile and flammable. Their vapors should not be inhaled or exposed to flame or sparks. Wear protective clothing on hands and arms and take care not to splash the solution into eyes or onto the face. Remember that water-repellent preservatives may contain toxic materials. Read all labels carefully.

Oils

Oils should be applied in the same way as semitransparent penetrating stains. Care should be used in handling cloths used to apply the oils.

CAUTION: Sponges or cloths that are wet with oils or oil-based stain are particularly susceptible to spontaneous combustion. To prevent fires, immerse the cloths in water or seal in an airtight container immediately after use.

Semitransparent Penetrating Stains

Semitransparent penetrating stains may be applied by brush, spray, pad, or roller. As with other finishes, brushing will usually give the best penetration and performance. Spray or roller application followed by back-brushing is also a good method of application. These oil-based stains are generally thin and runny, so application can be messy. Lap marks will form if stains are improperly applied (Fig. 41). Lap marks can be prevented by staining only a small number of boards or one panel at a time. This method pre-

Figure 41.—Lap marks on wood finished with semitransparent stain.

vents the front edge of the stained area from drying before a logical stopping place is reached. Working in the shade is desirable because the drying rate is slower. Stain that has been applied by spray without back-brushing is particularly prone to show blotchy patterns as it weathers (Fig. 42). One gallon will usually cover about 200 to 400 ft.^{2} of smooth surface and from 100 to 200 ft.^{2} of rough or weathered surface.

Two coats of penetrating oil-based stain on roughsawn or weathered lumber or plywood provide longer service-life than one coat, but only if the wood will accept the second coat. Apply the first coat to one panel or area. Then, work on another area so that the first coat can soak into the wood for 20 to 60 minutes. Next, apply the second coat before the first has dried. **If the first coat dries completely, the second coat cannot penetrate the wood.** Finally, about an hour after applying the second coat, use a cloth, sponge, or brush, lightly wetted with stain, to remove the excess stain. If this is not done, the stain that did not penetrate the wood will form an unsightly surface film and glossy spots. Stir the stain thoroughly during

Figure 42.—Lap marks formed by improper application of semitransparent penetrating stain.

application to prevent settling and color change. Avoid mixing different brands or batches of stain.

A two-coat system of oil-based stains on rough wood or plywood may last as long as 8 years. By comparison, one coat on new, smooth wood may last only 2 to 4 years. Although finished wood weathers much slower than unfinished wood, the semitransparent nature of oil-based stains permits some ultraviolet radiation to reach the surface. However, when the wood is refinished, the finish should last longer because the wood will accept more stain once it has weathered. The weathering rate of the stain is also affected by the density of the wood. Stain on wood such as western redcedar weathers faster than the same amount of stain on a denser wood such as Douglas-fir.

Latex semitransparent stains do not penetrate the wood surface, but they are easy to apply and less likely to form lap marks. These stains are essentially very thin paints and are not as durable as oil-based stains. A second coat will improve their durability. Apply the second coat any time after the first has dried. New formula-tions are being developed that may have some penetrating characteristics.

Transparent Film-Forming Finishes

Transparent film-forming finishes such as high-quality polyurethane or spar varnish are occasionally used for exterior applications, although their service life is limited. The wood surface should be clean and dry before the finish is applied. The wood should first be treated with a paintable water-repellent preservative (see subsection on Water-Repellent Preservatives in Chapter 6). The use of varnish-compatible, durable, pigmented stains and sealers or undercoats will help to extend the life of the finishing system. At least three top coats of varnish should be applied.

The life expectancy of transparent film-forming finishes on fully exposed surfaces is only 2 years at best. For optimal performance, apply many (up to six) thin coats of the finish (sand lightly between coats) and add a fresh coat each year. In marine exposures, six coats of varnish should be used for best performance.

7

● ●

SPECIAL APPLICATIONS

Several applications deserve separate discussion. These include the application of finish to decks, porches, fences, roofs, log structures, and structures in marine environments. In all of these applications, wood is exposed to particularly harsh weathering conditions. Special consideration should be given to finish selection and application. Log structures also need special consideration because of the large amounts of exposed end-grain and the deep checking associated with large timbers and logs.

Decks

Wood decks have become an important part of residential construction in recent years, and there is considerable confusion about how they should be finished. This confusion results from several factors: the use of preservative-treated wood, differences in preservatives, wide variety of species and grades of wood used, wide range of finishes available, and lack of understanding of wood properties. For optimal long-term performance, a wood deck should be maintained with a finish after construction. However, decks present a particularly severe exposure for wood

and finishes. Although a full range of both penetrating and film-forming finishes is available, penetrating finishes provide better overall performance and easier refinishing than do film-forming finishes.

Since wood decks may have full exposure to sun and rain, the weathering process is greatly accelerated. As wetting and drying occur, checks tend to enlarge into cracks, which allow water to easily penetrate deeply into the wood. The risk of decay and insect attack is greatly increased. The top surface of decking boards generally has a lower moisture content than the bottom of the boards. This is one of the reasons that decking boards cup. Cupping occurs whether the board is placed bark-side up or pith-side up. Film-forming finishes are subjected to excessive stress because of the continuous shrinking and swelling of the wood that results from changes in moisture content. Furthermore, the finish is subjected to abrasion, particularly in high-traffic areas.

Because decks can be fully exposed to weather, the lumber is usually pressure-treated with a waterborne preservative. Alternatively, naturally durable wood such as redwood or western redcedar is used for decking material. Although decks may be left to weather naturally, it is best to finish them.

Penetrating Finishes

Penetrating finishes are recommended for use on wood decks. These include water-repellent preservatives (unpigmented and pigmented) and semitransparent stains. Penetrating finishes are extremely effective in stopping the adsorption of liquid water, thereby decreasing dimensional changes in the wood. Less dimensional change results in less splitting, cracking, warping, and twisting and less stress on fasteners. These finishes enhance the appearance and service life of both naturally decay-resistant wood species and species pressure-treated with wood preservatives.

Some water-repellent preservatives are formulated with nondrying oils that act as solvents (such as paraffin oil). These oils penetrate the wood, but do not dry. They protect the wood from degradation and mildew attack just as other types of water-repellent preservative. Because the oils do not dry, the deck surface may remain oily until the finish absorbs. This usually takes several days but depends on the application rate and porosity of the wood.

Three manufacturers of waterborne preservative formulations are using a water repellent combined with chromated copper arsenate (CCA) treatment for 5/4 radial-edged decking. This lumber is currently marketed under the brand names Ultrawood, Wolman Extra, and Weathershield. Other similar products may be available. Research on even better combined formulations is continuing and these manufacturers will be marketing new products under the trade names Thompsonized, Weathergard, and Olympic Wood. This dual treatment gives the wood more resistance to weathering. Although the water repellent is supposed to thoroughly penetrate and saturate the wood, it is still advisable to treat the ends cut during construction with a water-repellent preservative. These treatments should improve wood characteristics and extend service life, particularly if the wood is periodically maintained with a water-repellent preservative.

A number of new finishes are being marketed both in waterborne and solventborne formulations that are lightly pigmented. These finishes penetrate the wood much like a traditional water-repellent preservative but tend to form a thin film. They permit most of the grain pattern of the wood to show, but color the wood slightly. The pigment extends the service life of the finish to about 2 to 3 years, compared to unpigmented water-repellent preservatives.

Semitransparent stains have a much higher concentration of pigments than do pigmented water-repellent preservatives, and the pigments are much coarser. The additional pigment provides color and greatly increases the durability of the finish compared to that of water-repellent preservatives. The binder in the stain absorbs into the wood surface just as with a water-repellent preservative, and there is no film formation.

If the decking material was given a factory-applied water repellent or if it was recently finished with a water-repellent preservative, a semitransparent stain may not absorb properly. In these situations, the wood should be allowed to weather for 2 to 3 months before finishing. This is the **only** situation where it is beneficial to wait this long before finishing wood with a penetrating stain. **Lumber should not be left unfinished for 6 months to a year as indicated by some product literature or as recommended by some paint and lumber suppliers.** A short drying period may sometimes be necessary (see subsection on Moisture Content in Chapter 6).

Film-Forming Finishes

Film-forming finishes cover a wide range of finishes from waterborne, latex-based semitransparent stains to paints and include both oil-based and latex solid-color stains (also called opaque or full-bodied stains). Almost all of these products are unsuitable for use on wood decks.

On structures fully exposed to the weather, such as decks, paints tend to trap moisture and can actually increase the decay hazard. The paint seal breaks at the joints between different pieces of wood (Fig. 43). These cracks permit entrance of water, which becomes trapped by the paint film. The trapped moisture leads to decay of untreated wood, and the paint will peel

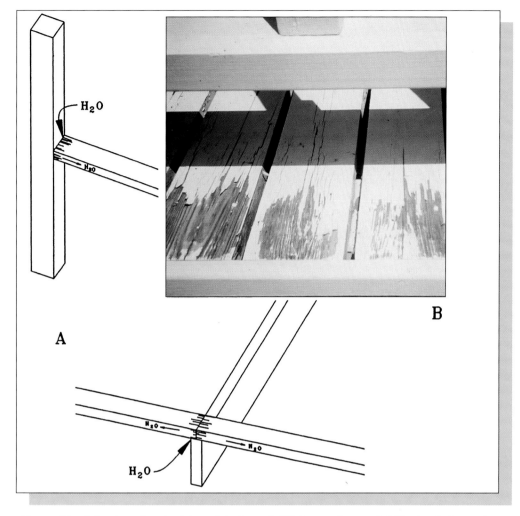

Figure 43.—Intrusion of water into painted wood. (A) Areas where paint film tends to crack; (B) paint failure caused by water intrusion.

at these joints. Proper pressure treatment with a preservative can eliminate the risk of decay. However, it is best to avoid the use of film-forming finishes on lumber that is fully exposed to the weather, even if the lumber has been pressure treated.

Methods for Finishing New Decks

The first finish on wood, whether it is a deck or any structure, is the most important. This finish should be applied as soon as the wood surface is dry. If the first finish is not applied properly, there is often little that can be done to correct problems that develop later. The choice between a penetrating and a film-forming finish should be considered carefully, because it is necessary to continue with that type of finish in the future. However, it is possible to use a film-

forming finish over a surface that was previously finished with a penetrating finish if the weathered surface is removed by sanding, wet sand blasting, or power washing.

If you decide to use a penetrating finish, the next decision is whether to use a semitranspar-

The easiest finish to maintain on a deck is a water-repellent preservative. The next easiest is a semitransparent, oil-based stain. Film-forming finishes, such as paints, are prone to fail by peeling and are not recommended. A water-repellent preservative requires frequent application, but the ease of refinishing compensates for the additional applications.

ent stain or a water-repellent preservative. The service life of a water-repellent preservative is about 1 year on exposed surfaces; however, water-repellent preservatives are extremely easy to reapply to decks. They absorb readily into the end grain of lumber and can stop water absorption into the end grain much longer than 1 year. Because water-repellent preservatives are generally not pigmented, problems with uneven wear and lap marks are eliminated.

If you are unsure whether to use stain or a water-repellent preservative, first apply a water-repellent preservative to the deck. It is possible to switch to a semitransparent stain when the deck needs to be refinished. Even if the deck has been maintained with a water-repellent preservative for many years, the semitransparent stain will perform satisfactorily because it penetrates the wood and will not fail by peeling as can a film-forming finish.

Railings around decks can be finished in the same way as the deck or as discussed in the section on fences. There is more flexibility in the finishes that can be used for the railing compared to the deck since the railing does not need the abrasion resistance of the finish used on the deck, and it can be designed to avoid trapping of moisture. Paints and solid-color stains may perform quite well on the railing. The railing should be designed to avoid exposure of the end-grain of the wood. The top of the railing can be designed like a mini-roof to protect the vertical parts (Fig. 44).

Methods for Cleaning Decks

The bright color of the wood on weathered decks can be restored by applying a commercial product called a deck cleaner, brightener, or restorer. Deck cleaners remove mildew and dirt and thus allow the natural color of the wood to

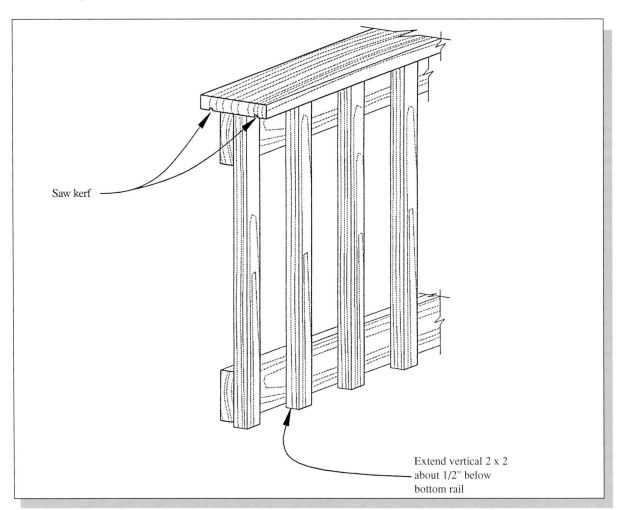

Saw kerf

Extend vertical 2 x 2 about 1/2" below bottom rail

Figure 44.—Construction of deck railing to protect end-grain of vertical pieces.
Note formation of drip-edge by saw kerf.

Figure 45.—Effect of brightener on portion of mildewed CCA-treated deck.

show (Fig. 45). They do not actually add color to the deck. If all of the natural color has been leached from the surface, the wood will appear silver-gray after cleaning. These products may remove the weathered wood surface, and some care should be exercised to avoid damaging the surface. Aggressive scrubbing with a caustic cleaner can actually remove surface wood, particularly on softer wood such as western redcedar. Mildew can also be removed using a liquid household bleach containing 5 percent sodium hypochlorite (see section on Mildew in Chapter 9). The bleach is usually diluted with water (1 part bleach, 3 parts water) before it is applied to the deck. The bleach solution should be rinsed from the deck with water. If the deck is to be finished after cleaning, allow 1 or 2 days of drying time.

Porches

Porches are protected by a roof, so the conditions are not as severe as those with decks; however, rain and sunshine exposure occur periodically and abrasive wear is similar to that on decks. Because porches are protected from rain, they can be finished with paint. There is still a fairly high risk of decay from trapped moisture, particularly at the base of pillars and posts, on railings, and at the outside portions of the floor. To improve the resistance to decay, the wood should be treated with a paintable water-repellent preservative prior to painting. Oil-based primers provide the best resistance to moisture. Primer and top coats should be formulated for use on porches because these formulations resist abrasion and wear. Because of their low resin content, solid-color stains should **never** be used on decks and porches. In high decay hazard areas, such as the southeastern United States, preservative-treated wood should be used (e.g., CCA-pressure-treated lumber).

Fences

Like decks, fences are fully exposed to the weather; moreover, at least some parts of fences are in contact with the ground. As a result, wood decay and termite attack are potential problems. Often, the design of fences does not take into consideration the protection of exposed end-grain. If a film-forming finish is to be used on a fence, it is extremely important to seal the end-grain and protect exposed end-grain wherever possible. Use lumber pressure-treated with preservatives for all posts and other parts of the fence that are in ground contact. Parts of the fence that are not in ground contact may be made from naturally durable species; however, pressure-treated wood will probably last longer than naturally durable wood.

Many fences are left to weather naturally. For resistance to decay and mildew, it is better to finish the wood with a water-repellent preservative. Apply the water-repellent preservative just before or just after construction, regardless of whether the lumber had been treated. Be sure to apply the preservative liberally to the ends of wood pieces and to those areas in which wood members come in contact with one another, because these areas are prone to trap moisture and then decay. Even with pressure-treated wood, surfaces that were cut during construction need to be treated with water-repellent preservative. Annual treatment may be necessary to prevent mildew. If mildew stains do develop, they must be removed before treatment (see subsection on Methods for Cleaning Decks in Chapter 7).

A water-repellent preservative will maintain the natural color of the wood for several years. Eventually, the extractives will leach out, and the wood will turn driftwood gray. Wood that has not been treated with a water-repellent preservative will turn gray because of mildew. This change usually occurs within several weeks. Unfortunately, the discoloration caused by mildew, while not damaging to the wood, is not always attractive. Black blotchy stains often develop.

Solventborne oil-based stains are recommended for fences, particularly if they are used in conjunction with water-repellent preservative. After treating the wood with a water-repellent preservative, allow the fence to weather for 2 to 12 months. Weathering time depends on the lumber. If roughsawn lumber is used, 2 months is probably enough time, although smooth-planed lumber will accept the stain better after a year of weathering. The stain should be formulated with a mildewcide and a water repellent.

Avoid solid-color stains (oil and latex), semi-transparent latex-based stains, and varnish on fences. The color and texture that such stains offer can be achieved with oil-based stains, without the disadvantage of peeling and increased risk of decay. Varnish lacks protection against ultraviolet radiation.

Film-forming finishes such as paint trap moisture and thus increase the risk of decay. However, for aesthetic reasons—such as the classic look of the white picket fence—paint can be used on fences. If you must paint the fence, it is best to use wood that has been pressure-treated with a preservative. Before painting, pretreat all surfaces that were cut during construction with a paintable water-repellent preservative; in fact, pretreating all the wood will improve both the service life of the paint and durability of the wood. If the wood is wet (e.g., pressure-treated wood that has not been kiln dried), let it weather for 2 to 3 weeks to allow it to dry before pretreatment. The wood should not be allowed to weather for 6 to 12 months as recommended by some suppliers. Excessive weathering causes surface degradation that will later weaken the paint bond. If pressure-treated wood is not used, use the heartwood of naturally decay-resistant species such as western redcedar or redwood. Pretreat the wood with a water-repellent preservative before painting. Wait 3 to 7 days after pretreatment to paint.

Alkyd primers provide the best resistance to moisture, but latex primers are more flexible. The primer for colored woods such as redwood and western redcedar must be a stain-blocking primer. Two top coats of acrylic latex should be applied over the primer. Allow 1 to 3 days drying time between coats and follow manufacturer's recommendations.

These guidelines are primarily focused on finishing smooth-planed lumber; however, the same procedures apply to roughsawn lumber. Roughsawn lumber will accept thicker paint coatings, which will extend the life of the finish.

Hot-dipped galvanized, stainless steel, or aluminum nails should be used for fences. Stainless steel nails are generally preferable to hot-dipped galvanized nails. For dense woods such as southern pine, hot-dipped galvanized nails are the best choice because some stainless steel and aluminum nails are soft and will bend when used on these species. Any of these corrosion-resistant nails will prevent rust stain and

Figure 46.—Structure with wood shingle roof and wood shake siding. Note the wide overhangs and gutters protecting the siding. (Photo courtesy of the Red Cedar Shingle and Handsplit Shake Bureau.)

blue-black discoloration in most circumstances. The more natural the finish, the more important the use of corrosion-resistant fasteners.

Roofs

Wood shingles and shakes are not the main roofing materials for most structures, but they do find widespread use in certain geographic areas and for some architectural styles (Figs. 46 and 47). Shingles are sawn from large blocks of wood, are tapered from one end to the other, and generally have a relatively smooth surface.

Shakes are split from larger blocks of wood and thus have a more rugged appearance. Shakes may be approximately the same thickness on both ends, or they may be sawn from corner to corner, thus providing taper as well as one relatively smooth side, which is turned down during installation. Shakes may also be grooved. Shingles and shakes are used for siding as well as roofs and may be treated with preservatives or fire retardants.

Wood Properties

Wood used in the manufacture of shingles should have the following properties: 1) durability, 2) freedom from splitting during nailing, 3) dimensional stability, i.e., low ratio of tangential to radial shrinkage and minimum shrinkage in all planes, 4) light weight, 5) good insulating properties, 6) adequate strength, 7) straight, even grain for ease of manufacture, 8) ability to accept stain, 9) ability to resist abrasion, and 10) pleasing appearance. Edge-grained shingles will perform much better than flat-grained. Western redcedar, redwood, cypress, and northern and southern white cedars all possess the desired properties, but nearly all commercial shingles are currently produced from western redcedar.

Durability is probably the most important consideration. The heartwood of old-growth western redcedar is rated as extremely durable. The generally small amount of sapwood associated with this species is nondurable. There is a general consensus that some second-growth timber, even of the decay-resistant species, is not as durable as the old growth. The durability of the wood is also decreased as rain or other sources of moisture leach the extractives from the wood. The heartwood extractives provide cedar with natural decay resistance. The average service-life of a cedar shingle roof is estimated to be about 10 to 15 years, whereas that of a shake roof is 15 to 20 years. These times will vary for different climates. Shakes have a longer service-life because less cross-grain is exposed, and therefore they are less prone to absorb water.

In addition to western redcedar, southern pine taper-sawn shingles may be available. Research has shown that this species can be

Figure 47.—Log house with wood shake roof.

manufactured into wood shingles and pressure treated with a wood preservative. A roof made with these kinds of shingles should be free of decay for 25 to 30 years. Other species may also be used for shingles if properly treated or naturally durable. A new process is currently under development to chemically treat other species for use as shakes and shingles. These treatments should improve dimensional stability and resistance to decay and fire.

Application of Shingles and Shakes

Regardless of the type of finish, if any, proper application of shingles and shakes is required for long service-life. Because roofs are directly exposed to moisture and rain, use only the top grade of shingles or shakes manufactured with edge-grained heartwood (or treated sapwood). Lower grades can be used on siding or where an undercourse is required. Some factors to consider when applying shingles are 1) the decking to which the shingles are nailed, 2) the number, location, and type of nails, 3) the head lap or amount of lap over the course below (which often depends on shingle grade and application), 4) the space between the edges of the shingles or shakes, and 5) the separation of edge joints from one course to another. The Red

Cedar Shingle and Handsplit Shake Bureau provides an excellent publication containing details on shingle and shake grades and application procedures. Similar information on CCA-treated Southern Pine shakes is available from the Southern Forest Products Association. (See Additional Sources of Information for addresses.)

Application of Finish

Shingles and shakes, whether used on a roof or as siding, are often left to weather naturally if they are made from a durable species such as western redcedar. Depending on exposure and climatic conditions, the wood generally turns silver, dark gray, or dark brown. However, in warm, humid climates common in the South and on heavily shaded roofs and siding, mildew, moss, algae, lichens, and even wood decay can occur with time. For these reasons and for aesthetic effects, various finishes and preservatives can be applied to wood shingles and shakes to obtain a particular color. The types of finishes used on siding may differ substantially from those used on roofs.

Weather will rapidly deteriorate any finishing system. Because large quantities of end-grain are exposed on shingles and shakes, the wood rapidly absorbs moisture, resulting in excessive shrinking and swelling. Because moisture tends to migrate from the living quarters to the outside of a house, shingles and shakes can also absorb moisture from their back side (adequate attic ventilation and vapor retarders should decrease this problem). Furthermore, when film-forming finishes are applied to in-place roofs, small dams of finish form across the bottom of the gaps between shingles, which adds to the amount of water absorbed by the back of the shingle.

As a result of these potential problems, film-forming finishes, such as paint, solid-color stains, and varnish, should **never** be used on roofs. A transparent finish such as varnish will deteriorate within a few months, whereas a pigmented finish such as paint will usually last only a few years. The result will be an unsightly appearance that is difficult to refinish. Increased wood decay is also likely because the film-forming finish can help to retain moisture in the shingle or shake. Paint and solid-color stains can be used on shake or shingle siding.

If roofs or siding are to be finished, penetrating oil-based stains provide the best performance. These stains provide color without entirely concealing the grain and texture of the wood. They are relatively long-lived and easily refinished and may last several years on roofs and considerably longer on siding. Rough-textured edge-grained surfaces provide longer service-life than do smooth surfaces. The stain should contain a wood preservative or a mildewcide. Some paints and stains are specially formulated for use on shingles. Those with the highest concentration of pigment will likely give the longest service-life. Water-repellent preservatives may also be used on roofs, but their life expectancy is only about 1 to 2 years.

The first coat of finish is best applied to shingles before they are installed so that the backs and end-grain as well as the faces are thoroughly coated. The finish may be applied by dipping the shingles to at least two-thirds their length and then standing them vertically until the finish has dried. Any additional coats may be applied by brushing or spraying after the shingles have been installed. Care should be taken to thoroughly coat the exposed end-grain with the finish, preferably by brushing. In addi-

tion to dipping, the finish may be applied by brushing, rolling, or spraying. Dipping is the most effective method, followed by brushing. If the backs are not finished, seepage of rainwater under the shingles may cause more curling than would otherwise take place. If a light-colored finish has been applied, the exposed end and edges of the shingles may be discolored by water-soluble extractives from the wood.

Preservatives and Fire Retardants

Where warm and humid conditions persist for substantial parts of the year, it is desirable to extend the life of wood shingles and shakes with pressure preservative treatments. Although any of the preservatives commonly used to pressure treat lumber could be used on shingles, the best performance can be achieved with chromated copper arsenate (CCA). The chromium in this formulation provides added protection against photodegradation. Many species and the heartwood of most species poorly absorb waterborne-preservative treatments. The manufacturer should certify through a third-party inspection agency that the shingles have the required retention and penetration of preservative. The same type of certification should be available for fire-retardant-treated shingles.

Maintenance

Leaves and other debris that often accumulate on roofs, particularly in roof valleys and gutters, will trap moisture in shingles, increasing the likelihood for decay. Therefore, loose debris should be routinely cleaned from roofs and gutters. Overhanging limbs and vines that provide excessive shade should also be removed.

The roof should be checked for moss or lichen growth and should be finished periodically with a water-repellent preservative to inhibit this growth. The single most effective method to prevent moss from developing on roofs is to use a zinc, galvanized steel, or copper ridge cap. The normal corrosion from these metals, when used as the ridge cap or stretched horizontally along the butt end of the shingles (every 4 to 6 feet down the roof with at least 1 inch exposed), will provide control of moss, mold, and mildew for decades. Treating the roof with selected chemicals can also provide protection. A solution of copper naphthenate with 3 to

Figure 48.—Deep checks on corners of old log structure retain moisture and encourage decay.

NOTE: Manufacturer's recommendations should be followed because wood preservatives can be toxic to plants and to humans if used improperly. Humans, animals, and vegetation should be protected from drippings and runoff from the roof or gutters.

4 percent metal content, copper octoate with 1 to 2 percent metal content, copper-8-quinolinate with about 1 percent active ingredient content, or other preservatives can be used to control moss, lichens, and surface decay and to prevent their growth for 1 to 3 years. Check the manufacturer's specifications. **Some of these preservatives are highly colored and may not be acceptable for certain uses.** Commercial formulations for roof treatment are available.

Regardless of the method used, treatments are limited to the surface of shingles. Treatments will not prevent decay within the shingle if the moisture content is conducive to

fungal growth. However, surface treatments can help to lengthen the life of a wood roof by retarding water absorption and preventing the growth of moss and lichens, which retain moisture in the wood and thereby promote wood decay. **The best method for assuring a long service-life for the roof is pretreatment with a water-repellent preservative or stain prior to installation and the incorporation of a copper ridge cap and/or copper strips into the roof.**

Before and during the 19th century, wood shingles, which were commonly used for roofs, were fastened to widely-spaced nailing strips without the use of tarred or asphalted felts as a secondary barrier. Today, asphalted felt is used as a secondary barrier over sheathing, so wood shingles typically dry less quickly. Providing an airspace between the shingles and the felt-covered sheathing vastly improves drying. The airspace can be accomplished by attaching furring strips to the felted roof deck parallel to the trusses or rafters and then attaching widely spaced nailers perpendicular to the furring strips. Water getting past the shingles can drain away, and the airspace allows drying. A commercial product called "Cedar Breather" is a thick plastic mesh that can be applied over roofing felt that creates some degree of airspace between the shingles and the felt-covered sheathing.

Log Structures

Interest in the construction of new log structures (Fig. 47) as well as maintenance and restoration of old ones has increased dramatically in recent years. These structures present some unique maintenance and finishing challenges. However, before a finish is even considered, the structure must be carefully built to keep the outside wood surface as dry as possible. Good design and construction practices include 1) adequate roof overhang with properly hung and maintained gutters and downspouts, 2) roof vents, 3) good drainage and ventilation around the foundation, 4) proper venting of showers, baths, and dryers, 5) adequate clearance between the soil and lower logs, and 6) proper log design so that any moisture will run down and off the log rather than become trapped. Trapped moisture is certain to result in wood decay. Old structures that are still sound were usually constructed with attention to moisture-proofing details. Also, naturally durable woods—such as heartwood of white oak, walnut, white pine, and cedar—were usually used, particularly for the lower courses of logs. However, even these woods will succumb to decay with prolonged exposure to moisture.

Log houses are particularly susceptible to decay because of the deep seasoning checks that occur in large logs. These checks allow moisture to penetrate the wood, which causes decay. Excessive end-grain is also exposed, particularly on the corners of log structures (Fig. 48). This end-grain as well as the notching of the logs allows for easy penetration of water. Proper construction, particularly wide roof overhangs, and the application of water-repellent preservative finishes can help decrease moisture absorption.

Because log houses are usually rustic in appearance, penetrating finishes are preferable to film-forming finishes. Water-repellent preservatives liberally applied every couple of years

NOTE: Most preservatives should not be used indoors. Always check manufacturer's recommendations and Material Safety Data Sheets for proper use of all preservatives.

will allow a new wood surface to weather to light brown or tan. The preservative will also help prevent decay should water penetrate the surface checks and cracks or end-grain. However, it will not prevent decay where poor construction practices allow repeated wetting or condensation. Deep surface cracks, lower courses of logs, joints between logs, corners of the structure, and bottoms of windows and doors often trap moisture and are particularly vulnerable to decay. Consequently, these areas should be maintained diligently.

Oil-based semitransparent stains containing a preservative and water repellent provide the same protection and last longer than water repellent preservatives alone. For new construction, apply the finish and preservative before chinking. In this way, the tops of the logs, which are particularly vulnerable to wetting and subsequent decay, can be treated and the chinking will not be inadvertently stained.

Application of a water-repellent preservative to weathered structures can help prevent further deterioration. Badly decayed logs and portions of logs should be replaced with sound wood. The new wood should be treated with a water-repellent preservative, and the source of moisture that caused the decay must be eliminated. To facilitate treatment of hard-to-reach areas that may have some decay, 1/4-inch holes can be drilled in the wood and filled, preferably several times, with preservative solution or boron rods that will diffuse into the adjacent wood. The holes should then be plugged with preservative-treated wood dowels.

The use of borates to control wood decay is a relatively new development in the United States and may be useful on log structures with moisture problems. The material is manufactured for brush or spray application or as a "rod" that can be inserted into holes bored in the wood. Borax can also be poured into the holes. The material diffuses through wet wood and provides protection against decay and wood-destroying insects. Since the borates diffuse through the wood and eventually leach from the wood, periodic retreatment is usually necessary. This material is available through distributors and can be applied by professionals such as pest control operators, log cabin manufacturers, and pole treaters.

Structures in Marine Environments

The marine environment is particularly harsh on wood finishes. The natural weathering process of wood and finishes is accelerated because of the abundance of moisture and exposure to sunlight. Wood fully exposed to a marine environment, especially if in contact with the water or soil, should be pressure treated with a wood preservative. The treatment should be based on applicable marine and in-ground use specifications, which have higher concentrations of preservatives. Such treated woods are not always paintable. However, wood treated with waterborne preservatives is paintable when clean and dry. Chromated copper arsenate (CCA) and similar waterborne formulations are the most paintable preservatives. Wood used in less decay-prone marine environments, such as boat houses, can be treated with a paintable water-repellent preservative, coated with a suitable paint primer, and top coated with at least two coats of quality, exterior finish. A water-repellent preservative used as the only finish will need to be refinished at least annually and often semiannually, depending on exposure conditions. Stains weather more rapidly in this environment than under less severe conditions.

Natural film-forming finishes (varnishes) for woods exposed to marine environments need almost constant care and refinishing. Use three to six coats of varnish for best performance. The application of a paintable water-repellent preservative or pigmented, varnish-compatible stain before finishing will help improve the performance of the varnish.

Wood used in salt or brackish water can also be damaged by marine borers (Fig. 49). Marine borers pose a serious threat to wood waterfront structures and have damaged wood ships throughout history. The marine borers that cause the greatest amount of damage can be divided into two main groups: Mollusca and Crustacea. Molluscs are shell animals like clams

Figure 49.—Extensive damage to a wood waterfront structure from marine borers (Limnoria).

and oysters. Molluscan borers are divided into two families, Teredinidae and Pholadidae. Teredinidae contains the genera *Teredo* and *Bankia*, commonly called wood-boring shipworms. Pholadidae includes the genus *Martesia* and resembles clams. This family is commonly referred to as Pholads or rock-boring piddock. Marine borers in the phylum Crustacea are related to lobsters and crabs. *Limnoria* and *Sphaeroma* are important wood-destroying genera in this group of borers. *Limnoria* are commonly referred to as gribbles.

Marine borers vary greatly in their distribution and ability to destroy wood. They are generally more destructive in tropical waters. Their population can rise and fall depending on any number of factors, such as salinity changes resulting from floods or other causes, water temperature, and dissolved oxygen content. There is some indication that marine borer populations are increasing with the decrease in pollution of marine environments. Because of the variation in marine borer population, consult local authorities before purchasing wood that will be placed in salt or brackish water.

8

REFINISHING OF WOOD

Exterior wood surfaces should be refinished as the old finish deteriorates. Wood may also be refinished for aesthetic reasons such as a change in color or type of finish; however, refinishing too frequently leads to excessive finish build-up and subsequent cracking and peeling. This usually occurs with many coats of paint, particularly with oil-based paints. Penetrating finishes tend to form films if refinished too often, and these films will appear shiny. In some cases, dirty painted surfaces can be cleaned by washing with a mild detergent and water. To achieve maximum service life from a refinished surface, conscientious surface preparation and finish application techniques should be followed.

Opaque Finishes

Pigmented, film-forming finishes (e.g., paints) block damaging ultraviolet radiation and protect the wood surface. The degradation of the film occurs at the film surface and results in slow erosion of the finish. This is the most benign mode of paint degradation because as the primer coat begins to show, another top-

coat can be applied. When painted wood is fully exposed to the weather, another type of degradation occurs. This degradation mode involves checking, cracking, and peeling, and it can occur with film-forming finishes. When paint has peeled, the surface of the wood is completely vulnerable to weathering. Paint peeling is the most serious mode of degradation.

In refinishing an old paint coat or a solid-color stain that has weathered normally, surface preparation and cleaning are essential for optimal performance of the new finish. **Note: special precautions are necessary if the old coating contains lead-based paint.** Be sure to follow necessary precautions for preparing the surface (see Chapter 11, Health and Environmental Considerations). Special precautions are necessary during paint removal, and the removed paint must be collected and disposed of as a hazardous waste. Surface preparation includes sanding the paint and weathered wood surface, as described in the following text. When working on lead-based paints this procedure should **not** be done without protective clothing and breathing apparatus approved by the Occupational Safety and Health Administration (OSHA). Paper dust-masks are **not** adequate protection.

To refinish the old surface, first remove all loose coating through scraping or power washing (see section on Removal of Finish in this Chapter). Sand any remaining coating to "feather" the edges smooth with the bare wood (Fig. 50). Feathering the edges of the paint and sanding the weathered surface of the wood allows the primer to adhere better, and the thickness of the primer and top coat will be more even than on an unfeathered surface. If not feathered, the new paint coatings will be thin at the ridge where the old paint film ends. This thin area will be the first place where the paint cracks, allowing water to penetrate to the wood where it will initiate peeling again. This is one reason why some surfaces need to be painted repeatedly. Again, special precautions are necessary if the old coating contains lead-based paint.

After scraping and feathering, scrub the remaining coating with a brush or sponge and water. Rinse the scrubbed surface with clean water. Wipe the surface with your hand. If the surface is still dirty or chalky, scrub it again with a detergent. Use a detergent only if necessary;

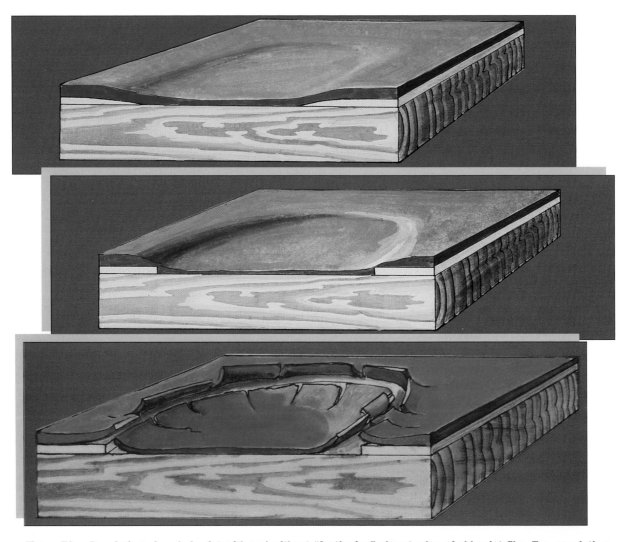

Figure 50.—Repainting of peeled paint with and without "feathering" abrupt edge of old paint film. Top, repainting with feathering. Thickness of new paint is consistent across boundary between old film and wood and is therefore more durable than the unfeathered finish. Middle, repainting without feathering. New paint is thin at abrupt edge of old paint film and (bottom) fails after a short time.

use the mildest conditions necessary to accomplish the cleaning. Note: Using too strong a detergent may leave a residue on the surface that will decrease the service life of the paint. Any mildew must be removed (see Mildew, Prevention and Removal in Chapter 9).

Rinse the cleaned surface thoroughly with water and allow it to dry before refinishing. If the surface is still chalky, it must be reprimed. Areas of exposed wood should be treated with a water-repellent preservative and allowed to dry for at least 3 sunny days and then primed. Remove any water-repellent preservative accidentally applied to coated areas. Apply one or two top coats. When refinishing with oil-based coatings, one top coat is usually adequate if the old surface is still in good condition.

It is particularly important to clean areas protected from sun and rain, such as porches and siding with wide roof overhangs. These areas tend to collect dirt and have mildew, which interfere with adhesion of the new coating. Protected areas, such as inside porches, sof-

fits, and on the north side of a building, seldom need to be refinished as often as those areas exposed to the weather. Simply washing protected areas will usually be sufficient, particularly areas finished with white or light-colored paints.

Latex paint can be applied to weathered painted surfaces if the old paint is clean and sound. The paintability of the surface can be tested with a simple procedure (Fig. 51). After cleaning the surface, refinish a small, inconspicuous area with latex paint, and allow it to dry at least overnight. Test for adhesion by firmly pressing one end of an adhesive bandage onto the painted surface. Then, quickly snap the bandage from the wood. If the tape is free of paint, the paint is well bonded, and the old surface does not need to be primed. If the paint adheres to the tape, the old surface is too chalky and needs priming with an oil-based primer. The primer should penetrate the old surface and form a firm base for the new coat of paint. If both the freshly applied paint and the old paint

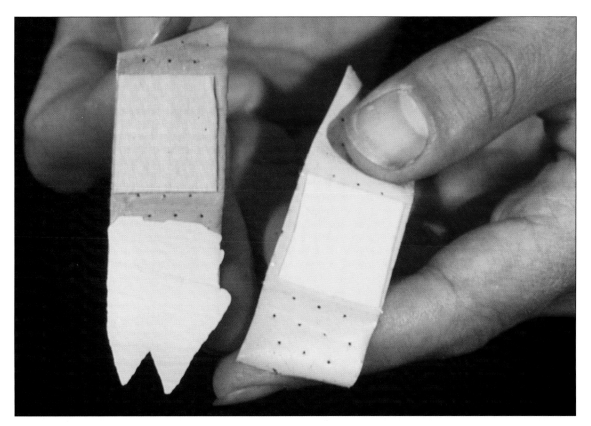

Figure 51.—Adhesive bandage test can be used to determine if a new coat of paint is properly bonded to an old surface. The bandage on the left was applied to a poorly bonded paint coat, the bandage on the right to a well bonded paint coat.

coat adhere to the tape, the old paint is not well-bonded to the wood and must be removed before repainting the surface.

Natural Finishes

The weathering of wood finished with penetrating finishes such as semitransparent stains and water-repellent preservatives is similar to that of unfinished wood. The surface of finished wood degrades, but at a slower rate than that of unfinished wood. Pigmented finishes (semitransparent stain) partially block sunlight. As the wood surface and the finish undergo simultaneous degradation, the pigment particles debond. As the pigment erodes from the surface, the wood becomes further degraded. To avoid excessive wood degradation, timely refinishing is essential.

> The surface should be refinished when pigment loss is evident. The subsequent finish should absorb into the wood. Finishing too early leads to inadequate absorption and film formation. Finishing too late allows for excessive wood degradation.

Water-Repellent Preservatives

Clean the old surface with a bristle brush to remove loose fibers and dirt, then apply the water-repellent preservative. It may be possible to clean the surface without water if it is not badly soiled or mildewed. If necessary, scrub the surface with a mild detergent solution. Before refinishing wood that had been finished with a water-repellent preservative, make sure that there is no mildew on the old surface. (See Mildew, Prevention and Removal in Chapter 9) Add bleach or another mildew remover to the detergent solution if necessary. Thoroughly rinse the surface and let it dry thoroughly before refinishing. The second coat of water-repellent preservative will last longer than the first because more finish soaks into the wood. The roughening of the surface combined with the development of small surface checks that are created by weathering enhances absorption of penetrating finishes.

To determine if a water-repellent preservative has lost its effectiveness, splash a small quantity of water on the wood surface. If the water beads up and runs off the surface, the treatment is still effective. If the water soaks in, the wood may need to be refinished. A water-repellent preservative sometimes breaks down at the surface but remains effective in protecting end-grain penetration of water. If the water seems to penetrate the wood quickly and deeply, the wood should probably be retreated with a water-repellent preservative. Refinishing is also required when the wood surface shows the blotchy discoloration caused by extractives or mildew.

Oils

Oil finishes can be refinished following the suggestions given for water-repellent preservatives.

Penetrating Stains

Penetrating stains are relatively easy to refinish. Excessive scraping and sanding are not required. Simply use a stiff bristle brush to remove all surface dirt, dust, and loose wood fibers, and then apply a new coat of stain. The second coat of penetrating stain often lasts longer than the first because the wood absorbs more stain.

Transparent Film-Forming Finishes

Transparent film-forming finishes, such as varnish, are not generally recommended for exterior use. If they are used, the refinishing

> **NOTE:** Steel wool and wire brushes should never be used to clean wood surfaces to be finished with stains, oils, or water-repellent preservatives because small iron deposits may be left on the surface. These deposits can react with certain water-soluble extractives in wood, particularly in species such as western redcedar, redwood, Douglas-fir, and the oaks, to produce dark blue-black stains.

practices described for opaque coatings should be followed.

Removal of Finish

The removal of paint and other film-forming finishes is a time-consuming and often difficult process. However, it is sometimes necessary for the preparation of a new surface if, for example, the old surface is covered with severely peeled or blistered paint or if cross-grain cracking has occurred because of excessive paint build-up. Finishes can be removed by sanding, wet sandblasting, spraying with pressurized water, electrically heated paint removers, and/or chemicals. Consult with local equipment-rental stores and paint dealers for available equipment, or request bids from professional contractors. **Before proceeding, be sure to review the section on the identification of health hazards associated with the removal of lead-based paints (see section on Lead-Based Paint, Chapter 11). Use of a blow torch is not recommended because of the fire danger and the volatilization of lead from lead-based paints.**

The removal of film-forming finish is also necessary if a penetrating stain or water-repellent finish is to be applied to a previously painted or stained (solid-color) surface. Changing from a film-forming to a penetrating finish sometimes does **not** give very good results. The wood surface is normally smooth and contains residual paint in the pores. This combination of residual paint and a smooth surface inhibits absorption of the stain or water-repellent preservative. In addition, the fasteners may not have sufficient corrosion resistance to perform well with penetrating finishes. The result is likely to be poorly finished, iron-stained wood.

Sanding

Disk, orbital, or siding sanders equipped with a tungsten carbide abrasive disk of medium grit are effective in removing old paint. This method is faster than others, and the tungsten carbide disk is less likely to clog compared to conventional sanding disks. The depth of cut for the sander can be set with the siding guide, but experienced operators often work freehand, without the guide. The operator should be careful to remove only the paint and not excess wood. After disk sanding, it is desirable to sand the surface lightly by hand or with straight-line power tool in the direction of the wood. Recent research has shown that surfaces prepared using 50 to 80 grit sandpaper provide better adhesion to finishes than do smooth-planed surfaces. **Sanding lead-based paint requires special precautions to ensure safety of workers, collection of dust, and disposal of hazardous waste. Sanding should not be attempted without these precautions.**

Wet Sandblasting and Pressurized Water Spray

Paint can also be removed by blasting with wet sand or using a high-pressure water spray. These methods usually require the services of a professional. The sand particles or water can erode the wood as well as strip the paint. The softer earlywood is eroded faster than the latewood, resulting in an uneven, rough surface. If proper care is taken to minimize damage to the wood, these methods can give a surface suitable for repainting. Wet sandblasting is faster than water blasting. For best results, the surface should be lightly sanded with 50 to 80 grit paper on the areas where the paint had peeled. Aggressive use of either wet sandblasting or pressured water spray may erode much earlywood from the surface, leaving a surface enriched in latewood that may not provide good adhesion to new paint. These rough surfaces may show through the new paint. The surface may not absorb stains or other penetrating finishes very well. Pressure in the range of

CAUTION: Some old paints contain lead, and sanding, sandblasting, or disturbing the surface in any way will release lead particles into the air. Inhalation of lead particles is detrimental to health. Be sure to review the information on lead-based paints in Chapter 11. Anyone sandblasting or using pressurized water spray equipment should wear approved eye goggles as well as a dust mask or respirator, as appropriate. Electrical equipment should be double-insulated and equipped with a three-wire grounded outlet having ground-fault protection.

approximately 1,000 to 2,000 lb./in.^{2} is typically used. Use the lowest pressure possible to remove the paint.

Electric Heat

Electrically heated paint removers can be used to remove paint. Heats softens the paint, causing it to separate from the wood. This method, although effective, is slower than sanding and requires at least a 1,000-watt heater to be effective.

Chemicals

Chemical paint and varnish removers are available commercially and are effective in removing all types of film-forming finishes and, to some extent, can partially remove penetrating stains. **Some of these products are caustic; the wood must be thoroughly neutralized and washed following their use. There have been problems reported with using these caustic strippers. In some cases, the surface must be sanded before using a film-forming finish because these chemicals actually pulp the wood surface.** The surface may be degraded in much the same way as occurs in weathering, and these surfaces cannot provide good paint adhesion. If the surface has been degraded by the paint stripper, penetrating finishes can be used without sanding. However, the surface should be properly neutralized and washed.

Chemical paint removers offer a distinct advantage to other methods if the paint film contains lead. This method is most conducive to containing, collecting, and disposing of the lead paint. The hazard from the lead is decreased, but there is considerable hazard from the chemical paint remover. The skin and eyes must be protected, and a breathing apparatus must be used.

9

DISCOLORATION OF WOOD AND FINISHES

The normal service life of a finish can be shortened in two ways: the finish itself can undergo degradation or it can become discolored. Although discoloration does not in itself constitute failure of a finish, the problem is often serious and requires remedial treatment. Discoloration can result from dirt, mildew, extractive bleed, wax bleed, exudation of pitch, iron stains, knots, water stains, and excessive chalking. Discoloration can occur independently of finish deterioration; although it can be unsightly, the finish can be quite sound and still provide protection to the wood. In some cases, cleaning the paint can solve the problem without repainting. In other cases, the discoloration is compounded by paint deterioration. Refinishing without correcting the original problem will result in repeated failure of the finish.

Dirt

The most benign cause of paint discoloration is the accumulation of dirt. This can be a bothersome problem on multi-story structures with large overhangs, but for most single-family residential structures periodic washing with a mild detergent will renew the paint. The problem is most noticeable on the ceilings of porches, soffits, and siding protected by large roof overhangs and porches. Adequate roof overhang of 2 to 4 feet is the best assurance to protect the structure from weathering, decay, and slight accumulation of dirt. The necessity for periodic cleaning is minor compared to problems caused by inadequate roof overhang.

Mildew

Mildew is probably the most common cause of discoloration of house paint, solid-color stains, and natural finishes (Fig. 52). It also causes the gray discoloration of unfinished wood. The term mildew applies both to the fungus (a type of microscopic plant life) and to its staining effects on the finish and the wood. Mildew fungi live on the paint or wood surface but do not "eat" the lignin or celluloses in the wood as do wood-rotting fungi. Because mildew fungi do not eat the wood, they degrade neither the wood nor the paint. Mildew fungi can use some extractives in wood and natural oils for

Figure 52.—Mildew on paint is most common in warm, humid climates. It also occurs in shaded or protected areas.

food. Wood species that contain an abundance of extractives tend to be more prone to mildew than other species. However, other factors such as surface roughness and the type of finish can have a greater effect. **Natural oils such as linseed oil and tung oil are food for mildew fungi. If these oils are applied to wood without a mildewcide, they can encourage mildew growth.**

The most common mildew is dark gray, but some is black, brown, red, green, or other colors. Mildew grows most extensively in warm, humid climates. Although mildew may be found anywhere on a building, whether or not the building is painted, it is most commonly found on walls behind trees or shrubs where air movement is restricted. Mildew may also be associated with areas where water splashes on the siding because of overflowing gutters or lack of gutters (Fig. 13). Dew will form on those parts of the house that are not heated and tend to cool rapidly, such as eaves, the ceilings of carports and porches, and the wall area between studs.

Mildew can be distinguished from dirt by examination under a 10-power magnifying glass. In the growing stage, when the paint surface is damp or wet, a mildew fungus is charac-terized by its threadlike growth. In the dormant stage, when the surface is dry, the fungus has many egg-shaped spores. By contrast, granular particles of dirt are irregular in size and shape. A simple test for the presence of mildew on paint and wood is to apply a drop or two of a fresh solution of household liquid bleach (5 percent sodium hypochlorite) to the stained area. The dark color of mildew will usually bleach out in 1 or 2 minutes. Discoloration that does not bleach out is probably dirt, extractives bleed, or iron stain.

As with dirty surfaces, washing will restore the appearance of a mildewed painted surface. However, this is a short-term solution because the mildew will grow back. Mildew is more difficult to remove from a stained surface because it infects both the surface of the wood and the stain. The stain prevents bleach from penetrating the wood. If the building does not need to be restained, application of a water-repellent preservative may help solve the problem. Restaining is not recommended to solve a mildew problem if the structure does not otherwise need to be restained. For painted structures, particularly in the southeastern United States, periodic washing may be necessary to keep the structure free of mildew. When it is time to repaint the structure, use a paint containing the best mildewcide possible. Some paint manufacturers put extra mildewcide in paints formulated for use in the southeastern United States.

Effect of Paint Composition

Paints and stains containing unmodified linseed oil are the most susceptible to mildew. Paints containing modified oils are less susceptible to mildew than unmodified oils, but mildew can still be a major problem in many areas. Mildew progresses more readily on exterior flat paint than on exterior semigloss or gloss enamel because the rougher surface of the flat paint makes it easier for the mildew to adhere to the surface. Of water-based paints, acrylic latex is the most resistant to mildew. Porous latex (water-based) paints without a mildewcide, applied over a linseed oil-based primer coat, will develop severe mildew in most climates, particularly in the warm humid climates common in the South.

A mildewcide (poison for mildew fungi) is often added to paint. The paint label should indicate if a mildewcide is present. If it is not, a mildewcide can sometimes be added by the local paint dealer. Note, however, that additions to a paint may interfere with curing and may void a manufacturer's warranty. Some paints are more vulnerable than others to attack by mildew. Zinc oxide, a common paint pigment in top coats, is not a mildewcide, but it does inhibit the growth of mildew.

The effectiveness of a mildewcide depends on the environment, wood species, type of paint, and pretreatment of the wood. Use of a water-repellent preservative as the first step in painting helps improve the mildew resistance of the paint (Fig. 53).

Prevention and Removal

For new wood surfaces in warm humid climates, mildew can be prevented by using top coats of paint containing zinc oxide and mildewcide over a primer coat that also contains a mildewcide.

Mildew must be removed before wood is refinished. If mildewed wood is refinished without cleaning the surface, the mildew can grow through the new coating. In this situation, it is usually impossible to control the mildew. The entire paint coat should be stripped and a new finish applied. Paint stores usually carry several brands of mildew cleaner. Some of these formulations contain sodium percarbonate; others contain sodium or calcium hypochlorite. These cleaners are very effective in removing mildew and cleaning the wood.

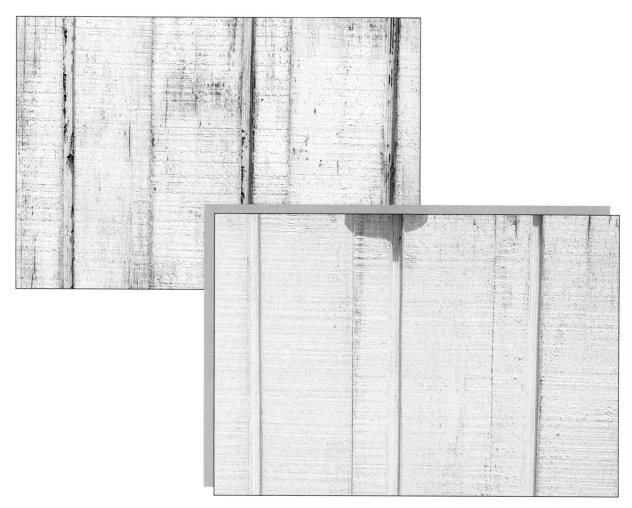

Figure 53.—Effect of pretreatment of wood with a water-repellent preservative prior to painting on the mildew resistance of paint. Top, untreated plywood panel; bottom, treated plywood panel.

Mildew Removal

Mildew can also be killed with a liquid household bleach solution. Scrub the painted surface with a bristle brush or sponge using the following solution:

$\frac{1}{3}$ cup household detergent

1 to 2 qt. (5 percent) sodium hypochlorite (liquid household bleach)

2 to 3 qt. warm water

This mixture can also be used to remove mildew from naturally finished or unfinished wood.

WARNING: Do not mix liquid household bleach with ammonia or with any detergents or cleansers containing ammonia. Bleach and ammonia form a lethal gas. Many household cleaners contain ammonia, so be extremely careful what type of cleaner is mixed with bleach.

Extractives Bleed

In some species, such as western redcedar, cypress, and redwood, the heartwood is dark because of the presence of water-soluble extractives. The extractives give these species their attractive color and natural decay resistance, but they can also discolor paint. The heartwood of Douglas-fir, white pine, and southern pine can also produce staining extractives, although the problem is not as severe as that encountered with western redcedar, cypress, and redwood.

When extractives discolor paint, moisture is usually the culprit. The extractives are dissolved and leached from the wood by water. The water then moves to the paint surface, evaporates, and leaves the extractives behind as a reddish-brown stain. Latex paints and the so-called breather or low-luster paints are more porous than are conventional paints and thus more susceptible to extractive staining.

Diffused Discoloration

Diffused discoloration from wood extractives is caused by rain and dew that penetrate a

Figure 54.—Diffused discoloration from bleeding of wood extractives.

porous or thin paint coat (Fig. 54). It may also be caused by rain and dew that penetrate joints in the siding or by water from faulty roof drainage and gutters, or it may be the result of paint with insufficient stain blocking properties. The discoloration will often follow the grain pattern and coloration of the wood (Fig. 55). Diffused discoloration is best prevented by following good painting practices.

Streaked Discoloration

Streaked discoloration or rundown can also occur when water-soluble extractives are pre-sent in the wood (Fig. 56). This discoloration results when the back of the siding is wetted, the extractives are dissolved, and the colored water runs down the face of the adjacent painted boards from the lap joint. Streaked discoloration can also result from the movement of water vapor within the house to the exterior walls and condensation during cold weather. Major sources of water vapor are humidifiers, clothes dryers and showers that are not vented to the outside, and moisture from cooking and dishwashing. Streaked discoloration may also be caused by water draining into exterior walls

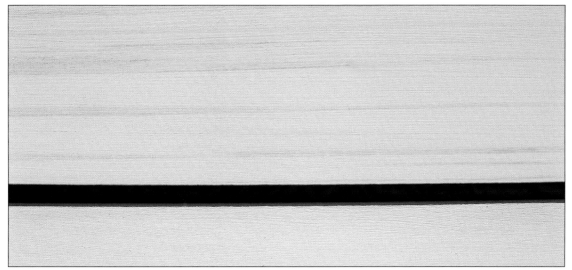

Figure 55.—Discoloration from extractive bleed will often follow the grain pattern of the wood.

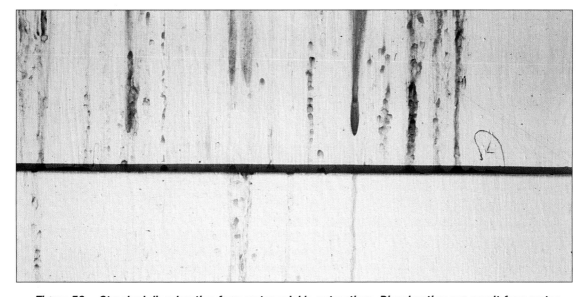

Figure 56.—Streaked discoloration from water-soluble extractives. Discoloration can result from water wetting the back of one piece of siding and then running down the front of the next piece.

from roof leaks, faulty gutters, or rain blown through louvers in vents. Rain water can be prevented from entering the walls by proper maintenance of gutters and roof.

Streaked discoloration can be prevented by eliminating condensation moisture in the walls. A vapor retarder (such as a continuous 6-mil polyethylene sheet) should be installed on the inside of all exterior walls in new or remodeled houses located in climate zones where winter condensation can occur in walls. If a vapor retarder is not practical, the inside of all exterior walls should be finished with a vapor-resistant paint. Water vapor in the house can be decreased by venting exhaust fans in bathrooms and kitchens to the outside. Clothes dryers should also be vented to the outside and not to the crawlspace or attic. If the house contains a crawlspace, the soil should be covered with a vapor retarder to prevent migration of water into the living quarters (see Chapter 2, Construction Practices).

Settings on humidifiers should be set low with consideration for both human comfort and durability of structural walls. The actual setting will depend on the outside relative humidity, temperature, and construction methods. A reasonable rule of thumb is to limit the indoor relative humidity to a level that will not produce condensation on windows.

To stop discoloration caused by extractives bleed, moisture problems must be eliminated. Streaked discoloration will usually weather away in a few months. However, discoloration in protected areas can become darker and more difficult to remove with time. In these cases, discolored areas should be washed with a mild detergent soon after the problem develops. Paint cleaners are also effective on darker stains. A solution containing 4 to 16 oz. of oxalic acid per gallon of warm water may also be effective.

Wax Bleed

The petrolatum wax used as a water repellent in some hardboard siding products may cause a discoloration problem called wax bleed. This problem can often be corrected by washing the affected surface with a detergent and water. For more severe cases, the surface should be reprimed and top coated after thorough washing and rinsing.

Exudation of Pitch

Pine and Douglas-fir can exude pitch (resin), and some cedar species can exude oils (see Fig. 5 and subsection on Extractives, Pitch, and Oils in Chapter 1). Pitch and oils should not ordinarily be a problem because lumber manufacturers have learned how to "set" pitch and evaporate excess oil during the kiln-drying process. However, if proper kiln schedules were not used to dry the lumber, the pitch and oils can exude from the wood.

When exudation occurs before the wood has been painted, the exuded materials should be removed. If the exuded pitch has hardened, it can be removed fairly easily with a putty knife, paint scraper, or sandpaper; however, if the pitch is still soft, such procedures smear it over the surface of the wood. If the pitch is not removed, the paint is likely to alligator, crack, and fail over the pitch-coated areas soon after painting. Soft pitch should be removed thoroughly by scrubbing the surface with cloths wet with turpentine or mineral spirits. After most pitch has been removed, the surface should be sanded. Heating the wood with a heat gun or other localized heat source can sometimes "set" or harden pitch.

If exudation occurs after the wood has been painted, the wood might best be left alone until it is time to repaint. The wood should then be scraped thoroughly before new paint is applied. If a few boards in the structure are particularly unsightly because of exudation or because of early paint failure, it may be wise to replace them with new lumber before repainting.

Exudation of pitch is exacerbated by high temperature. In extreme cases, boards have been known to continue to exude pitch for many years. Repainting should be deferred until all exudation has ceased or until repainting has become necessary for other reasons. No paints or painting procedures can be relied upon to prevent exudation of pitch.

Stains

Stains can result from mechanical and natural causes. In this section, iron stains, fungal blue stain, brown stain over knots, and water stain are discussed.

Iron Stains

Two types of stains are associated with iron. The red-brown discoloration caused by rust is associated with the use of ferrous nails and metal screens. Blue-black discoloration is caused by the reaction of wood extractives with iron and is associated with the use of ferrous nails and with iron traces from tools.

When standard ferrous nails are used on exterior siding and the siding is painted, a red-brown discoloration may appear through the paint in the immediate vicinity of the nailhead. To prevent rust stains, use corrosion-resistant nails. These include high-quality galvanized, stainless steel, and aluminum nails. The heads of poor-quality galvanized nails can be chipped when they are driven into the siding, corrode easily, and, like ferrous nails, cause unsightly staining of the paint. If rust is a serious problem on a painted surface, the nails should be countersunk and caulked, and the area should be spot primed and then top coated.

Rust stains may also occur when standard ferrous nails are used in association with other finishing systems such as solid-color or opaque stains, penetrating stains, and water-repellent preservatives. Rust stains can result when screens and other metal objects that are subject to corrosion and leaching are fastened to the surface of the building (Fig. 57).

An unsightly blue-black discoloration of wood can be caused by the formation of iron tannates. The iron reacts with certain wood extractives, such as tannins or tannic acid in species such as cedar, redwood, or oak. Ferrous nails and other iron or steel parts are the most common source of iron in chemical staining (Fig. 58), but problems have also been associated with traces of iron left from cleaning the wood surface with steel wool, wire brushes, or even steel tools. The discoloration can sometimes become sealed beneath the finish.

A solution of oxalic acid in water will remove blue-black discoloration provided it is not

> **WARNING:** Oxalic acid and its water solution are toxic and should be used with great caution.

already sealed beneath the finish. The stained surface should be given several applications of a solution containing about 1/2 lb. of oxalic acid per gallon of hot water. A saturated solution of sodium biflouride ($NaHF_2$) works as well but may be difficult to obtain. After the stains disappear, the surface should be thoroughly washed with fresh warm water to remove the oxalic acid and any traces of the chemical causing the stain. If all sources of iron are not removed or protected from corrosion, staining reoccurs.

Blue Stain

Blue stain is caused by microscopic fungi that commonly infect the sapwood of all woody species. Although microscopic, these fungi produce a blue discoloration of the sapwood (Fig. 59). Blue stain does not normally weaken wood structurally, but conditions that favor blue stain development are also ideal for serious wood decay and paint failure. When blue stain occurs, it is generally present throughout the sapwood and not just on the surface. Blue stain occurs primarily in the sapwood because of its high sugar content. The discoloration is permanent and is aggravated by additional wetting of the wood.

Wood in service may contain blue stain, and no detrimental effects will result as long as the moisture content is kept below 20 percent. Wood in properly designed and well-maintained houses has a moisture content of less than 20 percent. However, if the wood is exposed to moisture from rain, condensation, or leaky plumbing, the moisture content will increase, the blue stain fungi will develop further, and decay may even follow.

To prevent blue stain from discoloring paint, follow good construction and painting practices. First, do whatever is possible to keep the wood dry. Provide an adequate roof overhang, and properly maintain shingles, gutters, and downspouts. Window and door casings should slope away from the house, allowing water to drain away rapidly. In northern climates, use a

Figure 57.—Metal fasteners (top) or window screens (bottom) can corrode and later discolor paint as leaching occurs.

Figure 58.—Blue-black discoloration resulting from uncoated steel nails.

Figure 59.—Blue stain. Note that the stain penetrated through the sapwood of this cross-cut specimen.

vapor retarder on the interior side of all exterior walls to prevent condensation. Vent clothes dryers, showers, and cooking areas to the outside and avoid the use of humidifiers. Treat wood with a water-repellent preservative, then apply a nonporous mildew-resistant primer and at least one top coat of finish containing a mildewcide. If the wood has already been painted, remove the old paint and allow the wood to dry thoroughly. Apply a water-repellent preservative and repaint the wood.

A 5-percent solution of sodium hypochlorite (ordinary liquid household bleach) may sometimes remove blue-stain discoloration from the surface, but it is not a permanent cure.

Brown Stain Over Knots

The knots in many softwood species, particularly pine, contain an abundance of resin, which can sometimes cause paint to peel or turn brown (Fig. 8). In most cases, the resin is "set" or hardened by the high temperatures used in kiln drying of construction lumber.

Good painting practices should eliminate or control brown stain over knots. First apply a good primer to the bare wood and then apply two top coats. The primer should be recommended as good for blocking the extractives in the knot that can bleed through the finish. Specialty primer paints are available to seal knots for outdoor painting. Some manufacturers recommend a 4-lb.-cut orange shellac for controlling knot bleed. However, for exterior wood, shellac can sometimes cause wrinkling of the top coat, and shellac should be used with care. The use of varnish on the knot area may also result in early paint failure. These primer paints work best under high-quality acrylic latex top-coat paints. In fact, research has shown that a poor top-coat paint will negate the effects of a good primer paint for controlling knot bleed.

Water Stain

Wood siding can become water stained, particularly if it is left unfinished or if a natural finish has started to deteriorate. Water stains are most common at the base of siding where rainwater runs off a roof, hits a hard surface, and splashes onto the side of the building (Fig. 13). Water stains often occur in combination with extractive bleed and mildew growth. The water

causes the finish to deteriorate quickly in this area. If the finish is not replaced, the water can begin to remove the water-soluble extractives, which accelerates the weathering process, and the area becomes stained. Water stains can also be seen where gutters overflow. Good construction practices that keep water from contacting the wood should be followed whenever possible to prevent water stain. The wood should be treated regularly with a water-repellent preservative. Removing water stains can be very difficult. Sometimes scrubbing the wood with mild detergent and water is effective. Light sanding may be effective on smooth wood surfaces. Bleaches such as liquid household bleach or oxalic acid solutions have been used with varying degrees of success. Water stains are usually accompanied by mildew stains and extractive bleed.

Figure 60.—Chalking of paint. Chalking can discolor a lower surface as the resin and pigment particles wash down.

Chalking

Chalking is a property of the paint, not the wood. Chalking results when a paint film gradually weathers or deteriorates, releasing pigment particles. These particles act like a fine powder on the paint surface. Most paints chalk to some extent, which is desirable because chalking cleans the painted surface and is a normal consequence of weathering. However, chalking is objectionable when it discolors the surface (Fig. 60) or when it causes premature disappearance of the paint film through excessive erosion. With colored or tinted paints, chalking is a common cause of fading. The manner in which a paint is formulated may determine how fast it chalks. Therefore, if chalking is likely to be a problem, select a paint that the manufacturer has indicated will chalk slowly.

For repainting surfaces that have chalked excessively, proper preparation of the old surface is essential. Scrub the surface thoroughly with a detergent solution to remove all chalk deposits and dirt. Rinse thoroughly with clean water before repainting. To check for excessive chalking lightly rub the surface with a dark cloth (light colored paint) or a white cloth (dark colored paint). The amount of pigment removed by the cloth is a good indication of the chalking. The use of a top-quality oil-based primer or a stain-blocking acrylic latex primer may be necessary before latex top-coats are applied. Discoloration or chalk that has run down onto a lower surface may be removed by vigorous scrubbing with detergent and water. This discoloration will usually weather away gradually if the chalking on the painted surface has been corrected.

10

Degradation of Finishes

Unlike discoloration, which can occur almost anywhere on a structure, degradation of the paint film is usually limited to those areas exposed to the weather or water. Areas that deteriorate the fastest are those exposed to the greatest amount of sun and rain, usually on the south and west sides of buildings in the northern hemisphere.

Peeling and Cracking

Peeling From Substrate

Peeling of paint from the wood surface is usually caused by excessive water. In addition, film-forming finishes applied to weathered wood surfaces do not form strong adhesive bonds. Even in the absence of excessive water, these coatings may peel. See Chapter 4, Weathering of Wood, for a detailed description of the effects of weathering.

In some cases, the effects of water are fairly obvious (Fig. 61). Outdoor water sources include leaky roofs, ice dams, and lack of protection because of inadequate roof overhang. In other cases, the sources of water are not so obvious. Moisture from inside the building can migrate through gaps around windows and cause paint failure on trim (Fig. 62). Interior moisture can also cause paint failure on siding (Fig. 63). In Figure 63, note that peeling is most severe around the small window, which is probably in a bathroom. There is no paint failure outside the attic area. Sometimes, paint failure is most severe outside a single room (Fig. 64); note that the paint failure in this figure is under the porch, probably the result of moisture from inside the building. Paint failure quite often occurs outside of kitchens and bathrooms, particularly in older homes that lack vapor retarders. It is sometimes difficult to determine the source of the moisture. In Figure 65, the siding is protected from rain by an overhang. The source of the moisture is either condensation or migration of moisture from inside the structure. Painting over weathered wood often leads to widespread failure of the paint system (Fig. 66).

If paint has peeled, the source of water must be found and eliminated and the surface should be sanded prior to repainting.

Figure 61.—Paint peeling caused by exterior moisture.

Figure 62.—Paint peeling caused by interior moisture carried by air flow around window unit.

Intercoat Peeling

Intercoat peeling is the separation of the new paint coat from the old, which indicates that the bond between the two coats is weak (Fig. 67). This type of peeling can be prevented by good cleaning and painting practices. Intercoat peeling usually results from painting over severely chalked, mildewed, or dirty surfaces. Adequate cleaning of the weathered surface prior to repainting will remove the dirt and may remove enough chalk to provide good adhesion. As described in Chapter 8, Refinishing of Wood, the adhesive bandage test can be used to check adhesion (see Fig. 51). If cleaning does not lead to good adhesion, it may be necessary to prime the surface with an oil-based primer. Intercoat peeling generally occurs within 1 year of repainting. It can also occur on freshly painted wood if too much time elapses between application of the primer and top coat. If more than 2 weeks elapse before a top coat is applied to an oil-based primer, soaplike materials may form on the surface and interfere with the bonding of the top coat. When the period between applications exceeds 2 weeks, the surface should be scrubbed before applying the second coat. If the primer coat is applied in the autumn, do not

Figure 63.—Paint peeling caused by movement of interior moisture through wall.

Figure 64.—Paint can peel when excessive moisture moves through wall. Other forms of failure are also evident on this older house. (Photo courtesy of Southern Forest Products Association.)

wait until spring to apply the top coat. If the lapse in time is unavoidable, the surface should be washed and possibly reprimed before painting.

Cracking

Like peeling, cracking is usually caused by water; it normally precedes peeling. The cracking is aligned with the grain pattern of the wood and is exacerbated by raising of the grain. Cracking can be particularly severe on smooth plywood surfaces coated with alkyd paints. The cracks usually initiate with the lathe checks in the wood. These checks grow larger as the wood shrinks and swells through normal changes in moisture content and eventually cause enough stress in the paint to cause cracking. Alkyd paints are more prone to crack than latex paints because they are more brittle.

Cross-Grain Cracking

Cross-grain cracking occurs when paint coatings become too thick (Fig. 68). This problem often occurs on older homes that have been painted many times with oil-based paints. Paint usually cracks in the direction in which it was brushed onto the wood (i.e., with the grain). Cross-grain cracks run across the grain of the wood and paint. Once cracking has occurred,

Figure 65.—Failure of paint under overhang.

Figure 66.—Failure of paint applied to weathered wood.

Figure 67.—Intercoat peeling of paint is usually caused by poor preparation of the original surface.

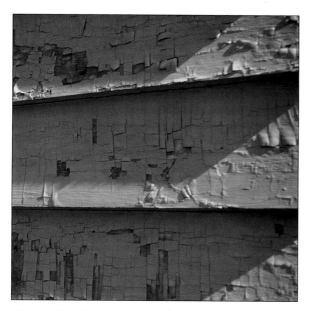

Figure 68.—Cross-grain cracking results from excessive build-up of paint.

the only solution is to completely remove the old paint and apply a new finishing system on the bare wood. It is fairly safe to assume that some paint that shows cross-grain cracking is lead-based paint. See precautions for removal of lead-based paint in Chapter 11.

To prevent cross-grain cracking, follow the paint manufacturer's recommendations for spreading rates. Do not repaint unweathered, protected areas such as porch ceilings and roof overhangs as often as the rest of the house. If possible, repaint these areas only as they weather and require new paint. Latex paints, based on either vinyl-acrylic or acrylic polymers, stay flexible throughout their service life and therefore do not fail by cross-grain cracking.

Blistering

Temperature Blisters

Temperature blisters are bubble-like formations that appear on the surface of paint films as early as a few hours or as long as 1 to 2 days after painting. They appear only on the last coat of paint (Fig. 69). The blisters occur when a thin, dry skin forms on the outer surface of the fresh paint, and the solvent in the wet paint under the skin changes to vapor and cannot escape. When the direct rays of the sun heat freshly painted wood, the rapid rise in temperature causes the vapors to expand and produce blisters. Only oil-based paints will blister in this way. Dark colors that absorb heat and thick paint coats are more likely to blister than are white paints or thin coats.

To prevent temperature blisters, avoid painting surfaces that will soon be heated. The best procedure is to "follow the sun around the house." The north side of the building should be painted early in the morning, the east side late in the morning, the south side well into the

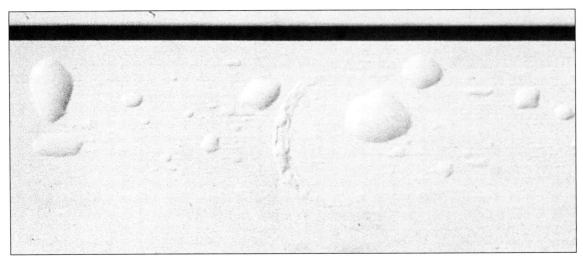

Figure 69.—Temperature blisters can form when partially dried paint is suddenly heated by direct rays of the sun.

afternoon, and the west side early in the morning or late in the afternoon. However, at least 2 hours should be allowed for the fresh paint film to dry before it cools to the point where condensation can occur. If blistering does occur, allow the paint to dry for a few days, scrape off the blisters, smooth the edges with sandpaper, and spot-paint the area.

Moisture Blisters

Moisture blisters are also bubble-like formations on the surface of the paint film. As the term implies, these blisters usually contain moisture when they are formed. Moisture blisters may occur where outside moisture such as rain enters the wood through joints and other end-grain areas of boards and siding. Moisture blisters usually occur on the wood surface. After the blisters appear, they dry out and collapse. Small blisters may disappear completely, but fairly large ones may leave a rough spot; in severe cases, the paint will peel. Thin coatings of new, oil-based paint are the most likely to blister. Old, thick coats are usually too rigid to swell and form blisters, so the paint will crack and peel instead.

Moisture may also enter wood because of poor construction and maintenance practices, particularly in the lower courses of siding. Paint failure is most severe on the side of a building

that faces the prevailing winds. Damage appears after spring rains and throughout the summer. Moisture blisters may occur on both heated and unheated buildings.

Moisture blisters may also result from the movement of water vapor from within the house to the outside. Plumbing leaks and improper venting of bath and kitchen areas, clothes dryers, and humidifiers are sources of inside water. If the interior side of outside walls does not contain a vapor retarder/air barrier, the moisture will move through the wall and cause moisture blisters or paint peeling. Such damage is not seasonal and occurs when the faulty condition develops.

Elimination of moisture and use of a vapor retarder and an air barrier are the best ways to prevent moisture blisters in paint. The moisture source should be identified and eliminated to avoid more serious problems such as wood decay (rot). If no obvious source of exterior moisture is found, decrease indoor moisture. Decrease the setting or shut off humidifiers, increase ventilation in the kitchen and bathrooms, and vent dryers to the outside. If the decrease in indoor humidity does not improve paint performance, placing 1/8-inch wedges between courses of siding sometimes provides enough ventilation to help eliminate paint peeling.

11

• •

Health and Environmental Considerations

Some finishing formulations used in the past and others that are still being manufactured and used are considered hazardous to health. Research on the toxicity of finishes is ongoing, and finishing formulations are in the process of change. Therefore, it is important to seek the most current information available from the manufacturer when choosing a finish.

EPA-Approved Information Sheets

The EPA-approved information sheets for each of the three major groups of wood preservatives are provided by producers to consumers of treated-wood products. These sheets, summarized here, provide users with information about the preservative and the use and disposal of treated-wood products. Anyone involved with preservative-treated wood products should become familiar with the information sheets and follow the advice therein.

Inorganic Arsenical Compounds, Pentachlorophenol, and Creosote

Consumer Information—Wood can be pressure-treated with a pesticide registered by the EPA that contains inorganic arsenical compounds, pentachlorophenol, and creosote as a protection against attack by insects and decay. Wood treated with these preservatives should be used only where such protection is important.

These preservatives penetrate deeply into and remain in the pressure-treated wood for a long time. Exposure to these preservatives may present certain hazards. Therefore, the following precautions should be taken both when handling the treated wood and in determining where to use or dispose of the treated wood.

Use Precautions—Do not use treated wood under circumstances where the preservative may become a component of food or animal feed. Examples of such sites would be structures or containers for storing silage or food.

Do not use treated wood for cutting-boards or countertops.

Only treated wood that is visibly clean and free of surface residue should be used for patios, decks, and walkways.

Do not use treated wood for construction of those portions of beehives that may come into contact with the honey.

Treated wood should not be used where it may come into direct or indirect contact with public drinking water, except for uses involving incidental contact such as docks and bridges.

Handling Precautions—Dispose of treated wood by ordinary trash collection or burial. Treated wood should not be burned in open fires or in stoves, fireplaces, or residential boilers because toxic chemicals may be produced as part of the smoke and ashes. Treated wood from commercial or industrial use (e.g., construction sites) may be burned only in commercial or industrial incinerators or boilers in accordance with State and Federal regulations.

Avoid frequent or prolonged inhalation of sawdust from treated wood. When sawing and machining treated wood, wear a dust mask. Whenever possible, these operations should be performed outdoors to avoid indoor accumulations of airborne sawdust from treated wood.

When power-sawing and machining, wear goggles to protect eyes from flying particles.

After working with treated wood, and before eating, drinking, or using tobacco products, wash exposed areas of skin thoroughly.

If preservatives or sawdust accumulate on clothes, launder before reuse. Wash work clothes separately from other household clothing.

Pentachlorophenol or Creosote Pressure-Treated Wood—Additional Considerations

Use Precautions—Logs treated with pentachlorophenol or creosote should not be used for log homes. Wood treated with pentachlorophenol or creosote should not be used where it will be in frequent or prolonged contact with bare skin (for example, chairs and other outdoor furniture), unless an effective sealer has been applied.

Pentachlorophenol- or creosote-treated wood should not be used in residential, industrial, or commercial interiors except for laminated beams or building components which are in ground contact and are subject to decay or insect infestation and where two coats of an appropriate sealer are applied. Sealers may be applied at the installation site. Urethane, shellac, latex epoxy enamel, and varnish are acceptable sealers for pentachlorophenol-treated wood.

Wood treated with pentachlorophenol or creosote should not be used in the interiors of farm buildings where there may be direct contact with domestic animals or livestock which may crib (bite) or lick the wood.

In interiors of farm buildings where domestic animals or livestock are unlikely to crib (bite) or lick the wood, pentachlorophenol- or creosote-treated wood may be used for building components which are in ground contact and are subject to decay or insect infestation and where two coats of an appropriate sealer are applied. Sealers may be applied at the installation site.

Do not use pentachlorophenol- or creosote-treated wood for farrowing or brooding facilities.

Do not use pentachlorophenol- or creosote-treated wood where it may come into direct or indirect contact with drinking water for domestic animals or livestock, except for uses involving incidental contact such as docks and bridges.

Handling Precautions—Avoid frequent or prolonged skin contact with pentachlorophenol- or creosote-treated wood. When handling the treated wood, wear long-sleeved shirts and long pants and use gloves impervious to the chemicals (for example, gloves that are vinyl-coated).

Lead-Based Paint

Lead-based paint was widely used in residential applications in the United States until the early 1940s. The introduction of different kinds of finishes led to a decline in the use of lead-based paint, although its use continued until 1976, particularly for the exterior of dwellings. In 1971, Congress passed the Lead-Based Paint Poisoning Prevention Act; in 1976, the Consumer Product Safety Commission (CPSC) issued a ruling under this Act that limited the lead content of paint used in residential dwellings, toys, and furniture to 0.06 percent.

Lead-based paint is still manufactured for applications not covered by the CPSC ruling, such as metal products, particularly those made of steel. Occasionally, such lead-based paint (for example, surplus paint from a shipyard) inadvertently becomes available to consumers through retail stores. A study conducted for the Environmental Protection Agency in 1986 indicated that about 42 million U.S. homes still contain interior and/or exterior lead-based paint. The increase in the rehabilitation of such homes has raised growing public and official concern about how to abate the toxicity of lead-based paint.

Studies have shown that ingestion of even minute amounts of lead can have serious effects on health, including hypertension, fetal injury, and damage to the brain, kidneys, and red blood cells. Low levels of ingestion can also cause partial loss of hearing, impairment of mental development and IQ, growth retardation, inhibited metabolism of Vitamin D, and disturbances in blood formation. The American Academy of Pediatrics regards lead as one of the foremost toxicological dangers to children.

Lead-based paint applied to the exterior of homes disintegrates into chalk and powder as a result of the effects of moisture and ultraviolet radiation. This extremely fine lead dust can accumulate in the soil near the house and can ultimately enter the house. Poor quality lead-based paint used on interior surfaces can also produce dust. Lead dust can be generated when coatings on surfaces are broken through aging or as a result of rehabilitation. The dust cannot be completely removed by conventional housecleaning methods.

The methods used to abate the toxicity of lead-based paint or to remove the paint can themselves generate lead dust. This is particularly true when unacceptable methods and work practices are used. Poorly performed abatement can be worse than no abatement at all. The micron-sized lead dust particles can remain airborne for substantial periods and cannot be fully removed by standard cleaning methods from the surfaces on which they have settled. When working on old painted surfaces, the worker should assume that one or more of the paint coats contain lead. Proper precautions should be taken accordingly.

Paint coats may be checked for lead content. A portable x-ray fluorescence (XRF) analyzer is commonly used to determine the level of lead in paint. Because this device has the potential for giving very inaccurate results if used by an unexperienced person, the analysis should be done by a qualified professional. Chemical spot testing, using a solution of 6 to 8 percent sodium sulfide in water, is sometimes used to screen painted surfaces for the presence of lead. Be certain to check all paint coats as the older ones are more likely to be lead based. A kit for detecting lead-based paint is available from the Civil Engineering Laboratory, Naval Construction Battalion Center, Port Hueneme, California 93043. Other sources of information are available from Lead Harm 1-800-435-LEAD and Laboratory Test System, 621 Grant St., Silverton, Oregon 97381.

The removal of lead-based paints can present some serious health problems. The Department of Health and Urban Development (HUD) has taken a leading role in developing guidelines for the removal of lead-based paints. At this time, HUD has approved three approaches to abating the toxicity of lead-based paint:

1. Covering the painted surface with wallboard, a fiberglass cloth barrier, or permanently attached wallpaper.
2. Removing the paint by scraping or heat treatment.
3. Replacing the entire surface to which lead-based paint has been applied.

Different strategies for abating the toxicity of lead-based paint are described in Tables 6 and 7. Certain practices are prohibited in houses owned and operated by HUD: machine sanding without an attached high-efficiency particulate air (HEPA) vacuum filtration apparatus, use of propane torches, uncontained waterblasting, washing, and repainting.

WARNING: Remodeling or refinishing projects that will require disturbing, removing, or demolishing portions of the structure that are coated with lead-based paint pose serious problems. The home dweller should seek information, advice, and perhaps professional assistance for addressing these problems. Contact HUD for the latest information on the removal of lead-based paints. Debris coated with lead-based paint is regarded as hazardous waste.

Table 6—Advantages and disadvantages of toxicity abatement strategies.

Abatement strategy	Advantage	Disadvantage

Replacement	Upgrade of finish possible
	Permanent solution
	Low risk of failure to
	   meet clearance standards
		Replacement possibly
		   lower in quality than
		   original component
		Creation of hazardous waste
		Skilled labor required
		   for installation

Encapsulation	Minimal generation of dust
	Rapid installation
		Protection possibly limited
		   to short term
		Routine inspection required
		Expert installation required
		   for product durability
		Routine maintenance
		   possibly required

Onsite paint
removal
	Restoration possible
	Low level of skill required
		High generation of dust
		Difficult-to-remove lead
		   residue left on substrate
		Moderate risk of failure to
		   meet clearance standards
		   and to protect workers
		Use of hazardous stripping
		   agents

Offsite paint
removal
	Restoration possible
	Finished product generally
	   superior to that produced
	   by onsite paint removal
		Difficult-to-remove lead
		   residue left on substrate
		Potential damage to product
		   during removal from site
		   and reinstallation

Table 7—Applications for toxicity abatement strategies.

Abatement strategy	Appropriate applications	Inappropriate applications

Replacement	Exterior and interior
	   components
	Substitution for deteriorated
	   component
	Windows, doors, and easily
	   removed building
	   components
		Restoration projects
		Most walls, ceilings, and
		   floors
		When historic trust
		   requirements apply

Encapsulation[a]	Exterior trim, walls, and floors
	Interior floors, walls,
	   ceilings, and pipes
	Balustrades
		Inappropriateness of
		   encapsulant for substrate
		   and conditions
		Repainting of leaded
		   surfaces, recovering with
		   paper/wallpaper

Onsite paint[b]	Limited surface areas Substitution for impractical abatement methods Metal substrates	Large surface areas

Offsite paint[c]	Restoration projects,
	   especially doors, mantels,
	   and easily removed trim
	Metal railings
		Some stripping procedures
		   inappropriate for metal

[a] Durability essential. Seams must be sealed to prevent escape of lead dust. Safe, effective, and aesthetic encapsulants for interior trim components need to be developed and tested.
[b] Check with manufacturer about recommendations for use on various types of wood and metal substrates.
[c] Check with stirpping company for timing of work and procedures of neutralizing and washing components.

Removal of lead-based paint by scraping or application of heat does not solve the problem of lead-particulate dust. Scraping should be accompanied by misting. Dry scraping is prohibited by Maryland abatement regulations. Sanding without a HEPA-filtered vacuum should not be used as a finishing method after scraping or any other method of toxicity abatement. The HEPA sanders are recommended for limited surface areas only; they are most appropriate for flat surfaces such as door jambs and stair risers. Open abrasive blasting is also prohibited by some regulations. The use of heat-based removal methods or paint strippers is recommended for limited surface areas.

High levels of airborne lead can be produced by heat guns, and the use of respirators is essential. Some lead is likely to be volatilized at the operating temperatures of most heat guns. Lead fumes are released at about 700°F. Heat guns capable of reaching or exceeding this temperature should not be operated in that range.

Chemical methods for removing lead-based paint may require multiple applications, depending on the number of paint coats. Caustic and solvent-based chemicals should not be allowed to dry on the lead-painted surface. If the chemicals dry, paint removal will not be satisfactory and the potential for creating lead dust will be increased.

Chemical substances used for paint removal are usually hazardous and should be used with great care. Some solvent-based chemical strippers are flammable and require ventilation. They may contain methylene chloride, a central nervous system depressant that is a possible carcinogen and that at high concentrations can cause kidney and liver damage. Supplied-air respirators should be used when working with strippers containing this substance. If the solvent-based strippers do not contain methylene chloride, organic vapor filters must be added to respirators. Caustic chemical strippers also have a very high pH (alkaline content), which can cause severe skin and eye injuries.

CONCLUSIONS

The wide range of wood and wood-based materials and the variety of paints, stains, and other finishes give the consumer tremendous latitude and flexibility for protecting a structure. Proper protection begins with good design of the structure, followed by good construction practices. The choice of materials must be made in concert with the design, good understanding of the materials being used, and knowledge about the weather conditions that will affect the structure. This is particularly true for the siding and finish used on the siding. In many cases there is no "right" method for the selection and application of siding and finish. The information in this manual should help the consumer make knowledgeable decisions about selecting and applying finishes to siding and other types of exterior wood.

ADDITIONAL SOURCES OF INFORMATION

Cassens, D.L., B.R. Johnson, W.C. Feist, and R.C. De Groot. 1994. Selection and use of preservative-treated wood. Forest Products Society, Madison, WI.

Consumer Reports. 256 Washington St., Mount Vernon, NY 10550.

Feist, W.C. 1983. Finishing wood for exterior use. In: Carter, R.M., ed. Finishing Eastern Hardwoods. Forest Products Society, Madison, WI, pp. 185-198.

Feist, W.C. 1987. Weathering performance of finished yellow-poplar siding. *Forest Products Journal* 37(3):15-22. Forest Products Society, Madison, WI.

Feist, W.C. 1988. Weathering performance of finished southern pine plywood siding. *Forest Products Journal* 38(3):22-28. Forest Products Society, Madison, WI.

Feist, W.C. 1990. Outdoor wood weathering and protection. In: Rowell, R., ed. *Archaeological wood, properties, chemistry, and preservation.* Chapter 11, Advances in Chemistry Series 225. American Chemical Society, Washington, DC.

Forest Products Laboratory. 1987. Wood handbook: Wood as an engineering material. Agric. Handb. 72. (Rev.). U.S. Department of Agriculture, Washington, DC.

Forest Products Society. 2801 Marshall Court, Madison, WI 53705.

Gorman, T.M. and W.C. Feist. 1989. Chronicle of 65 years of wood finishing research at the Forest Products Laboratory. Gen. Tech. Rep. FPL-GTR-60. U.S. Department of Agriculture, Forest Service, Forest Products Laboratory, Madison, WI.

Ingram, L.L., Jr., G.D. McGinnis, P.M. Pope, and W.C. Feist. 1983. Effect of coating systems on the vaporization of pentachlorophenol from treated wood. Proceedings, 79th annual meeting, American Wood Preservers Association 79:32-41.

Kropf, F.W., J. Sell, and W.C. Feist. 1993. Comparative weathering test of North American and European wood finishes. Report 115/27, Swiss Federal Laboratories for Materials Testing and Research, Duebendorf, Switzerland.

Lstiburek, J. and J. Carmody. 1991. Moisture Control Handbook: New, low-rise, residential construction. Oak Ridge National Laboratory, Oak Ridge, TN.

McDonald, K.A., R.H. Falk, R.S. Williams, and J.E. Winandy. 1996. Wood Decks: Materials, construction, and finishing. Forest Products Society, Madison, WI.

Red Cedar Shingle and Handsplit Shake Bureau. 515 116th Avenue NE, Suite 275, Bellevue, WA 98004.

Ross, A.S. and W.C. Feist. 1991. The effects of CCA-treated wood on the performance of surface finishes. Proceedings, annual meeting of American Wood Preservers' Association 87:41-55.

Ross, A.S., S. Bussjaeger, R. Carlson, and W.C. Feist. 1992. Professional finishing of CCA pressure-treated wood. *American Painting Contractor* 69(7):107-114

Southern Forest Products Association. P.O. Box 52468, New Orleans, LA 70152.

Williams, R.S. 1991. Effects of acidic deposition on painted wood: A review. *Journal of Coatings Technology* 63(800):53-73.

Williams, R.S., J.E. Winandy, and W.C. Feist. 1987. Adhesion of paint to weathered wood. *Forest Products Journal* 37(11/12):29-31. Forest Products Society, Madison, WI.

Williams, R.S. and W.C. Feist. Water repellent and water-repellent preservative finishes for wood. *Forest Products Journal*, in press. Forest Products Society, Madison, WI.

GLOSSARY

Air-dried lumber — Lumber that has been dried by placing it outdoors in stacks having spacers (stickers) between the layers.

Alkyd-based paint — Synthetic paint resins formed by modifying vegetable oils, such as linseed oil. Sometimes referred to as oil-based paint, although this is not strictly correct.

Annual growth ring — The growth layer put on a tree in a single growth year, including springwood and summerwood.

Back brushing — Brushing a wet paint or stain that has been applied by another method, such as sprayer or roller, to work the finish into the wood and even out the finish.

Back priming — Priming the back side of wood siding.

Bark — Outer layer of a tree, comprising the inner bark, or thin, inner living part (phloem) and the outer bark, or corky layer, composed of dry, dead tissue.

Batten — A narrow strip of wood used to cover joints or as decorative vertical members over plywood or wide boards.

Blind-nailing — Nailing in such a way that the nailheads are not visible on the face of the work. Blind-nailing is usually done at the tongue of matched boards.

Blue stain — A bluish or grayish discoloration of the sapwood caused by the growth of certain dark-colored fungi on the surface and in the interior of wood. It is difficult to remove because it can occur throughout the sapwood.

Bow — The distortion in a board that deviates from flatness lengthwise but not across its face.

Brown stain — (1) A rich brown to deep chocolate-brown discoloration of the sapwood of some pines caused by a fungus that acts much like the blue-stain fungi. (2) A chemical discoloration of wood, which sometimes occurs during the air drying or kiln drying (especially high temperature drying) of wood, apparently caused by the concentration and modification of extractives. (3) Resins from knots bleeding through paint. (4) Bleed-through of water soluble extractives through paint.

Cambium — The one-cell-thick layer of tissue between the bark and wood that repeatedly subdivides to form new wood and bark cells.

Caulk — (1) To fill or close a joint with a seal to make it watertight and airtight. (2) The material used to seal a joint.

Cell — A general term for the minute units of wood structure, including wood fibers, vessels members, and other elements of diverse structure and function.

Cellulose — The carbohydrate that is the principal constituent of wood and forms the framework of the wood cell.

Check — (1) A lengthwise separation of the wood, usually extending across the rings of annual growth and commonly resulting from stresses set up in the wood during seasoning. (2) Small separations in the lateral surface of wood that occur parallel to the grain. (3) Small separations in the surface of a paint film caused by weathering of the paint surface. Checks should not be confused with cracks, that originate in the substrate, and extend through the full thickness of the paint film.

Checking — (1) The process of forming checks. (2) Fissures that can appear with age in exterior paint coatings. Such fissures, at first superficial, may in time penetrate entirely through the coating to form cracks.

Chinking — The material used to or process to seal the space between logs in log structures.

Clear wood — Wood that has no knots.

Coalescence — The film formation process for latex finishes. As the water evaporates from a latex finish the individual emulsion particles fuse to form a film.

Coalescing agent — A high boiling point solvent incorporated into latex finishes to soften the polymer in the latex emulsion thus enhancing coalescence (film formation).

Condensation — The formation of liquid water from water vapor. Beads or films of water, or frost in cold weather, that accumulate on the inside of the exterior covering of a building when warm, moisture-laden air from the interior reaches a point where the temperature no longer permits the air to sustain as vapor the moisture it holds. Dew formation.

Corner board — A board used as trim for the external corner of a house or other frame structure, against which the ends of the siding are butted.

Counterflashing — A flashing usually used on chimneys at the roofline to cover shingle flashing and to prevent moisture entry.

Course — A continuous horizontal arrangement of blocks, bricks, siding boards, or shingles.

Cove molding — A molding with a concave face used as trim or to finish interior corners.

Cracks — (1) Large openings in wood that run parallel to the grain and extend deeply into the wood, sometimes through many growth rings. (2) Openings in paint that extend throughout the paint film to the wood surface and sometimes into the wood substrate as well. See also Check and Lathe check.

Crawl space — A shallow space, normally enclosed by the foundation walls, below the first floor of a structure that has no basement.

Crook — The distortion in a board that deviates edgewise from a straight line from end to end of the board.

Cup — The distortion in a board that deviates flatwise from a straight line across the width of the board.

Cupping — The process of forming cup in a board.

Decay — Degradation of wood or other biological materials through the action of fungi, as opposed to insect damage and/or weathering. *Advanced (or typical) decay.* The older stage of decay in which the destruction is readily recognized because the wood has become punky, soft and spongy, stringy, ring shaked, pitted, or crumbly. Decided discoloration or bleaching of

the rotted wood is often apparent. *Incipient decay.* The early stage of decay that has not proceeded far enough to soften or otherwise perceptibly impair the hardness of the wood. It is usually accompanied by a slight discoloration or bleaching of the wood.

Deck paint — An enamel with a high degree of resistance to mechanical wear, designed for use on such surfaces as porch floors.

Deformed shank nail — A nail with ridges on the shank to provide better withdrawal resistance.

Density — The mass of substance in a unit volume. When expressed in the metric system, it is numerically equal to the specific gravity of the same substance.

Dewpoint — Temperature at which a vapor begins to deposit as a liquid. Applies especially to water in the atmosphere.

Diffuse-porous wood — Certain hardwoods in which the pores tend to be uniform in size and distribution throughout each annual ring or to decrease in size slightly and gradually toward the outer border of the ring.

Dimensional stabilization — Controlling the swelling and shrinking of wood (caused by changes in its moisture content with changes in relative humidity) through special treatments.

Downspout — A pipe, usually of metal, for carrying rainwater from roof gutters.

Dressed and matched — See Tongue and groove.

Drip — (1) A structural member of a cornice or other horizontal exterior-finish course that has a projection beyond the other parts for water runoff. (2) A groove in the underside of a sill or drip cap to cause water to run off on the outer edge.

Drip cap — A molding placed on the exterior top side of a door or window frame to cause water to run off beyond the outside of the frame.

Dry rot — A term loosely applied to any dry, crumbly rot but especially to that which, when in an advanced stage, permits the wood to be crushed easily to a dry powder. The term is actually a misnomer, since all wood-rotting fungi require considerable moisture for growth.

Dry weight — The weight of wood that has no water absorbed. Ovendry wood.

Drying oil — An oil capable of reacting with atmospheric oxygen to form a solid film.

Earlywood — See Springwood.

Edge-grained lumber — See Grain, Edge-grained lumber.

Edgenailing — Nailing into the edge of a board.

End-grained — See Grain, End-grained.

End-nailing — Nailing into the end of a board which results in very poor withdrawal resistance.

Equilibrium moisture content (EMC) — The moisture content at which wood neither gains nor loses moisture when surrounded by air at a given relative humidity and temperature.

Extractives — Substances in wood, not an integral part of the cellular structure, that can be removed by solution in hot or cold water, ether, benzene, or other solvents that do not react chemically with wood components.

Face-nailing — Nailing perpendicular to the initial surface being penetrated. Also termed direct nailing.

Facia — A flat board, band, or face, used by itself or, more often, in combination with moldings, generally located at the outer face of the roof.

Fiber saturation point — The stage in the wetting or drying of wood at which the cell walls are saturated and the cell cavities are free from water. It applies to an individual cell or group of cells, not to whole boards. It is usually taken as approximately 30 percent moisture content, based on ovendry weight.

Fiberboard — A broad generic term inclusive of sheet materials of widely varying densities manufactured or refined or partially refined wood (or other vegetable) fibers. Bonding agents and other materials may be added to increase strength, resistance to moisture, fire, or decay, or to improve some other property.

Fiber (wood fiber) — A comparatively long (one twenty-fifth or less to one-third inch), narrow, tapering wood cell closed at both ends.

Flashing — Sheet metal or other material used in roof and wall construction to prevent water entry into adjoining parts of the structure.

Flat paint — An interior paint that contains a high proportion of pigment, and dries to a flat or lusterless finish.

Flat-grained lumber — See Grain, Flat-grained lumber.

Flatsawn — See Grain, Flat-grained lumber.

Fungi — Microscopic plants that live in damp wood and cause mold, stain, and/or decay.

Fungicide — A chemical that is poisonous to fungi.

Fur out — To place thin strips of wood (1/4 to 3/4 inch thick) over the sheathing or insulation board to create an air space behind siding.

Furring — Strips of wood or metal applied to a wall or other surface to even it and to serve as a fastening base for finish material.

Gable — The portion of the roof above the eave line of a double-sloped roof.

Gloss paint, gloss enamel — A paint or enamel that contains a relatively high proportion of resin compared with the pigment (a finely ground pigment) and dries to a high sheen or luster.

Grain — The direction, size, arrangement, appearance, or quality of the elements in wood or lumber. To have a specific meaning the term must be qualified.

Close-grained wood. Wood with narrow, inconspicuous annual rings. The term is sometimes used to designate wood having small and closely spaced pores, but in this sense the term "fine textured" is more often used.

Coarse-grained wood. Wood with wide conspicuous annual rings in which there is considerable difference between springwood and summerwood. The term is sometimes used to designate wood with large pores, such as oak, ash, chestnut, and walnut, but in this sense the term "coarse textured" is more often used.

Cross-grained wood. Wood in which the fibers deviate from a line parallel to the sides of the piece. Cross grain may be either diagonal or spiral grain, or a combination of the two.

Edge-grained lumber, vertical-grained lumber, quartersawn lumber. Lumber that has been sawn so that the wide surfaces extend approximately at right angles to the annual growth rings. Lumber is considered edge grained when the rings form an angle of 45° to 90° with the wide surface of the piece.

End-grained. The grain as seen on a cut made at right angle to the direction of the fibers (e.g., on a cross section of a tree).

Flat-grained lumber, flatsawn lumber. Lumber that has been sawn so the wide surfaces extend approximately parallel to the annual growth rings. Lumber is considered flat grained when the annual growth rings make an angle of less than 45° with the surface of the piece.

Open-grained wood. Common classification by painters for woods with large pores, such as oak, ash, chestnut, and walnut. Also known as "coarse textured".

Green — Freshly sawn lumber, or lumber that has received no intentional drying; unseasoned. The term does not apply to lumber that may have become completely wet through waterlogging.

Gutter, eave trough — A shallow channel or conduit of metal, vinyl, or in some cases wood, set below and along the eaves of a house to catch and carry off rainwater from the roof.

Hardwoods — Generally, the botanical group of trees that have broad leaves, in contrast to the conifers or softwoods which have needlelike or scalelike leaves. The grouping of trees into hardwoods is done on the basis of anatomical differences in the structure of the wood. The term has no reference to the actual hardness of the wood. The highest and lowest density wood species are both hardwoods.

Heartwood — The wood extending from the pith to the sapwood, the cells of which no longer participate in the life processes of the tree. Heartwood may be infiltrated with gums, resins, and other materials that usually make it darker and more decay resistant than sapwood.

Heavy-bodied stain — See Opaque stain.

Hemicellulose — Celluloses formed by the polymerization of sugars other than glucose (the monomer for cellulose).

Humidifier — A device designed to increase the humidity within a room or a building by means of the discharge of water vapor. Humidifiers may consist of individual room-size units or larger units attached to the heating plant to condition the entire building.

Joist — One of a series of parallel structural members, usually 1-1/2 inches in thickness, used to support floor and ceiling loads, and supported in turn by larger beams, girders, or bearing walls.

Juvenile wood — Wood formed during the early years of a trees growth (usually the first 8 to 10 years) that has unusual properties. Juvenile wood tends to shrink and swell much more, in the longitudinal direction, with changes in moisture content, than does normal wood.

Kerf — A cut made by a saw in a piece of wood.

Kiln-dried lumber — Lumber that has been dried by means of controlled heat and humidity, in ovens or kilns, to specified ranges of moisture content. See also Air-dried lumber.

Latewood — See Summerwood.

Latex paint — A paint containing pigments and a stable suspension, in water, of synthetic resins (produced by emulsion polymerization) that forms an opaque film through coalescence of the resin during water evaporation and subsequent curing.

Laquer — A fast drying finish comprised of a polymer dissolved in a very volatile solvent. Lacquers are usually unpigmented when used on wood and are used to finish furniture.

Lathe check — Small cracks that occur parallel to the grain in veneer as it is cut from the log. As unfinished plywood weathers, these checks can initiate cracking throughout the surface veneer. They can also initiate cracking of paint films, particularly oil- or alkyd-based paints.

Lignin — The main noncarbohydrate component of wood consisting of approximately 30 percent of its volume that is found primarily between wood fibers and cells. It is the natural adhesive that bonds the fibers and cells together in woody plants. Chemically, it is an irregular polymer of substituted propylphenyl groups, and no simple chemical formula can be written for it. Its phenolic nature makes it less stable to ultraviolet radiation from sunlight than the cellulosic components of wood.

Linseed, linseed oil — A drying oil extracted from the seeds of the flax plant (*Linum usitatissimum*) that is used in the paint industry to produce a wide array of resins for use in formulating oil-based finishes. The oil is a mixture of several triglycerides of fatty acids. The high percentage of esters of linolenic and linoleic acids, which contain a high degree of unsaturation, give the oil its rapid drying ability. The drying occurs through an air oxidation at the double bonds to crosslink the oils to form a polymeric film. The drying time of the oil can be improved and the viscosity increased through several processes to give blown oil, bodied oil, or boiled oil.

Blown oil. A drying oil that has been partially oxidized (polymerized), to increase its viscosity, by blowing air through it at elevated temperatures.

Bodied oil. A drying oil that has been partially polymerized, to increase its viscosity, usually by heating.

Boiled oil. A drying oil that has been processed by heating, heating with compounds of colbalt and/or manganese to form acid salts, or adding soluble driers.

Lumber — General term for wood that has been cut to standard widths, thickness, and length.

Dimension lumber. Lumber from 2 inches to, but not including, 5 inches thick and 2 or more inches wide. Includes joists, rafters, studs, planks, decking, and small timbers.

Pressure-treated lumber. Lumber that has had a preservative chemical forced into the wood under pressure to resist decay and insect attack.

Mil — One one-thousandth of an inch. The thickness of a paint film is usually measured in mils in the United States.

Mildew — A decay organism that can live on the paint and/or wood surface. Mildew is not a decay fungi and therefore cannot degrade wood. It does, however, grow better under moist conditions, and can indicate conditions favorable for decay fungi. Mildew can metabolize the nonstructural components of wood such as extractives and resins. Mildew can also metabolize natural oils such as linseed oil and tung oil, particularly if they have not been modified to improve curing. Linseed oil applied to redwood is extremely prone to develop black mildew stains.

Millwork — Building materials made of finished wood and manufactured in millwork plants and planing mills. It includes such items as inside and outside window and door frames, blinds, mantels, panels, stairways, molding, and interior trim. The term does not include flooring or siding.

Mineral oil — See Paraffin oil.

Mineral spirits — A petroleum distillate used as a solvent and thinner for oil-based paints, stains, varnishes, and similar products.

Moisture content — The amount of water contained in wood, expressed as a percentage of the total weight of the wood in an ovendry state (see Ovendry wood). See also Air-dried lumber and Kiln-dried lumber.

Natural finish — A transparent finish which does not seriously alter the original color or obscure the grain of the natural wood. Natural finishes are usually provided by sealers, oils, varnishes, water-repellent preservatives, and other similar materials.

Naval stores — A term applied to the oils, resins, tars, and pitches derived from oleoresin contained in, exuded by, or extracted from trees chiefly of the pine species (genus *Pinus*) or from the wood of such trees.

Oil-based paint, oil paint — A paint that contains a drying oil or modified drying oil as the component that polymerizes to form a film. See Alkyd-based paint.

Oil-based stain, oil stain — A stain that contains a drying oil or modified oil, in an organic solvent such as mineral spirits, that penetrates the wood's surface before it cures. Used correctly, these stains do not form films on the wood surface.

Old growth — Timber growing in or harvested from a mature, naturally established forest. When the trees have grown most or all of their individual lives in active competition with their companions for sunlight and moisture, this timber is usually straight and relatively free of knots.

Opaque stain, heavy-bodied stain, solid-color stain — A film-forming finish that is more like a paint that a stain. They are available in both oil-based and latex formulations and form a film rather than penetrate into the wood like a true stain.

Open-grained wood — See Grain, Open-grained wood.

Oriented standboard (OSB) — A type of structural flakeboard composed of layers, with each layer consisting of compressed strand-like wood flakes aligned in one direction, and with the layers oriented at right angles to each other. The flakes and layers are bonded together with a phenolic resin.

Ovendry wood — Wood dried to constant weight in an oven at temperatures above that of boiling water (usually 101°C to 105°C or 214°F to 221°F).

Paint — (1) To apply a finish. (2) A pigmented liquid that can be applied to a surface that converts to an opaque solid film after application.

Paraffin oil, paraffinic, mineral oil — A liquid component from petroleum having the consistency of oil.

Paraffin wax — A solid component from petroleum comprised of long chain alkanes that have melting points in the range of 54°C to 80°C.

Particleboard — Panels composed of small wood particles usually arranged in layers without a particular orientation and bonded together with a synthetic resin. Some particleboards are structurally rated. See also Structural flakeboard.

Penny — As applied to nails, it originally indicated the price per hundred. The term serves as a measure of nail length and is signified by the letter d.

Photochemical degradation — The degradation of wood and/or finish surfaces catalyzed by the ultraviolet radiation in sunlight.

Pitch pocket — An opening that extends parallel to the annual growth rings and that contains, or has contained, either solid or liquid pitch.

Pitch streak — A well-defined accumulation of pitch in a more or less regular streak in the wood of certain softwoods.

Pitch — (1) A component in the wood of some softwoods. It is a sticky viscous solution of rosin dissolved in turpentine. Its viscosity is dependent on the amount of turpentine that it contains and the temperature. Pitch can be "set" (i.e., solidified) in wood by using appropriate kiln schedules to drive off the turpentine. (2) The measure of the steepness of the slope of a roof, expressed as the ratio of the rise of the slope over a corresponding horizontal distance. Roof slope is expressed in the inches of rise per foot of run such as 4 in 12.

Pith — The small, soft core at the original center of a tree around which wood formation takes place. Also the small, soft core occurring in the structural center of a branch or twig.

Plainsawn lumber — Another term for flat-grained lumber. See Grain, Flat-grained lumber.

Plywood — An assembly made of layers (plies) of veneer, or of veneer in combination with a lumber core, joined with an adhesive. The grain of adjoining plies is usually laid at right angles, and almost always an odd number of plies are used to obtain balanced construction.

Pore — See Vessels.

Porous woods — Another name for hardwoods, which frequently have vessels or pores large enough to be seen readily without magnification.

Preservative — Any substance that is effective, for a reasonable length of time, in preventing the development and action of wood-rotting fungi, borers of various kinds, and harmful insects that deteriorate wood.

Primer — The first coat of paint system that consists of two or more coats; also the paint used for such a first coat.

Quartersawn lumber — Another term for edge-grained lumber usually used for hardwood lumber. See Grain, Edge-grained lumber.

Rabbet — A rectangular longitudinal groove cut in the corner edge of a board or plank.

Rays, ray cells — Strips of cells extending radially within a tree and varying in height from a few cells in some species to 4 or more inches in oak. The rays serve primarily to store food and transport it horizontally in the tree.

Relative humidity — The amount of water vapor in the atmosphere, expressed as a percentage of the maximum quantity that the atmosphere could hold at a given temperature. The amount of water vapor that can be held in the atmosphere increases with the temperature.

Resin passage, resin duct — Intercellular passages that contain and transmit resinous materials. On a cut surface, they are usually inconspicuous. They may extend vertically parallel to the axis of the tree or at right angles to the axis and parallel to the rays.

Reverse board and batten, plywood finish — Siding in which narrow battens are nailed vertically to wall framing and wider boards are nailed over these so that the edges of boards lap battens. A slight space is left between adjacent boards. This pattern is simulated with plywood by cutting wide vertical grooves in the face ply at uniform spacing. This plywood is sometimes referred to as Texture 1-11 (T 1-11).

Ring shank nail — A nail with ridges forming rings around the shank to provide better withdrawal resistance.

Rosin — The natural resin found in many trees after removal of the volatile fractions. A component of pitch.

Rot — Degradation of wood caused by decay fungi. See Decay.

Sap — All the fluids in a tree except special secretions and excretions, such as pitch.

Sapwood — The outer zone of wood in a tree, next to the bark. In the living tree it contains the living cells (the heartwood contains none). In most species, it is lighter colored than the heartwood. In all species, it lacks resistance to decay.

Sealer — A finishing material, either clear or pigmented, that is usually applied directly over uncoated wood to seal the surface.

Semigloss paint or enamel — A paint or enamel made with a slight insufficiency of nonvolatile vehicle so that its coating, when dry, has some luster but is not very glossy.

Semitransparent stain — A stain that allows some of the wood surface properties to show.

Latex semitransparent stain. A water borne stain that forms a thin layer on the wood's surface. This thin layer allows some of the wood surface characteristics to show.

Oil-based semitransparent stain. See Oil-based stain.

Shake — (1) A thick handsplit shingle, resawn to form two shakes; usually edge-grained. (2) A separation along the grain of wood, usually occurring between the annual growth rings. Also called ring shake.

Sheathing paper — A building material, generally paper or felt, used in wall and roof construction as a protection against the passage of air and water.

Sheathing — The covering used over joists, studs or rafters of a structure, usually available in 4 by 8 foot sheets.

Shellac — A transparent coating made by dissolving lac, a resinous secretion of the lac bug (a scale insect that thrives in tropical countries, especially India), in alcohol. It is primarily for indoor use because it has little resistance to water. It has good resistance to resinous wood extractives and is therefore used to seal knots.

Shingles — Roof covering of asphalt, fiberglass, asbestos, wood, tile, slate, or other material or combinations of materials such as asphalt and felt, cut to stock lengths, widths, and thicknesses.

Siding — The covering on the outside wall of a frame building, whether made of horizontal or vertical boards, shingles, shakes, or other materials.

Bevel siding, lap siding. Wedge-shaped (end view) boards used as horizontal siding in a lapped pattern. Bevel siding varies in butt thickness and is commonly available in widths up to 8 inches.

Drop siding. Siding that is usually 3/4-inch thick and 6 or 8 inches wide, with tongue-and-groove or shiplap edges.

Shiplap siding. Siding that has been milled along the edge to make a close rabbeted or lapped joint. It is usually used for siding.

Sill — (1) The lowest member of the frame of a structure, resting on the foundation and supporting the floor joists or the uprights of the wall. (2) The member forming the lower side of an opening such as a door sill or window sill.

Soffit — The underside of an overhanging cornice.

Softwoods — Generally, the botanical group of trees that bear cones and in most cases have needlelike or scalelike leaves; also the wood produced by such trees. The term has no reference to the actual hardness of the wood but is classified according to its anatomical characteristics.

Solid-color stain — See Opaque stain.

Specific gravity — The ratio of the weight of a body to the weight of an equal volume of water at 4°C or other specified temperature.

Springwood, earlywood — The portion of the growth ring that is formed during the early part of the growing season. It is usually less dense and weaker than summerwood.

Stain — (1) A discoloration in wood that may be caused by such diverse agents as microorganisms, metal, or chemicals. (2) Materials used to color wood.

Structural flakeboard — A panel material made of specially produced flakes which are compressed and bonded together with an exterior grade synthetic resin. Popular types include waferboard and OSB (oriented strandboard). Structural flakeboards are used for many of the same applications as plywood.

Structural lumber. Lumber that is 2 or more inches thick and 4 or more inches wide, intended for use where working stresses are required. The grading of structural lumber is based on the strength of the piece and the use of the entire piece. See also Lumber.

Stud — One of a series of slender wood or metal vertical structural members placed as supporting elements in walls and partitions.

Studwall — A wall consisting of spaced vertical structural members with thin facing material applied to each side.

Summerwood, latewood — The portion of the annual growth ring that is formed after the springwood formation has ceased. In most softwoods and all ring-porous hardwoods, it is denser and stronger mechanically than springwood.

Tangential — Strictly, coincident with a tangent at the circumference of a tree or log, or parallel to such a tangent. In practice, however, it often means roughly coincident with a growth ring. A tangential section is a longitudinal section through a tree or limb and is perpendicular to a radius. Flat-grained and plainsawn lumber is sawn tangentially.

Tannic acid, tannin — An organic acid found in many woody plants. It reacts with iron to form a dark bluish-black stain.

Texture 1-11, T 1-11 — See Reverse board and batten.

Tongue and groove — Boards or planks machined in such a manner that there is a groove on one edge and a corresponding projection (tongue) on the other edge, so that a number of such boards or planks can be fitted together. "Dressed and matched" is an alternative term with the same meaning.

Tracheids — The elongated cells that constitute the greater part of the structure of the softwoods (frequently referred to as fibers). Also present in some hardwoods.

Trim — The finish materials in a building, such as molding applied around openings (window trim, door trim) or at the floor and ceiling of rooms (baseboard, cornice, and other moldings).

Tung — A drying oil usually obtained from *Aleurites fordii* or *montana*. It contains a high percentage of elaeostearic acid in its triglycerides, which has three conjugated double bonds, and therefore dries quickly compared with other drying oils.

Turpentine — A colorless volatile liquid distilled from sap obtained from some pines that can be used as the solvent for oil-based finishes. It was formerly used extensively in paints but now has been largely replaced by mineral spirits.

Varnish — A thickened preparation of drying oil or drying oil and resin, suitable for spreading on surfaces to form continuous, transparent coatings, or for mixing with pigments to make enamels.

Vehicle — The liquid portion of a finishing material; it consists of the binder (nonvolatile) and volatile thinners.

Vertical-grained lumber — See Grain, Edge-grained lumber.

Vessels — Wood cells of comparatively large diameter that have open ends and are set one above the other so as to form continuous tubes. The openings of the vessels on the surface of a piece of wood are usually referred to as pores.

Virgin growth — The original growth of mature trees.

Volatile organic compounds (VOCs) — Volatile compounds in finishes such as mineral spirits, turpentine, and coalescing agents and/or in wood such as turpentine and certain extractives.

Volatile thinner — A liquid that evaporates readily, that is used to thin or reduce the consistency of finishes without altering the relative volumes of pigments and nonvolatile vehicles (e.g., turpentine and mineral spirits).

Waferboard — A type of structural flakeboard made of compressed, wafer-like wood particles or flakes bonded together with an exterior grade synthetic adhesive. The flakes may vary in size and thickness and may be either randomly or directionally oriented.

Wane — Bark, or lack of wood from any cause, on the edge or corner of a board. Hence, waney.

Warp — Any variation from a true or plane surface. Warp includes bow, crook, cup, and twist, or any combination thereof.

Warping — Process of forming warp.

Water repellent (WR) — A liquid designed to penetrate into wood, to impart water resistance. It is used for millwork such as sash and frames, and is usually applied by dipping. WRs may also be brush applied as a penetrating natural finish or as a pretreatment for painting.

Water-repellent preservative (WRP) — A liquid designed to penetrate into wood, to impart water resistance and moderate preservative protection. It is used for millwork such as sash and frames, and is usually applied by dipping. They may also be brush applied as a penetrating natural finish or as a pretreatment for painting.

Weathering — Photochemical degradation of the surface of wood or finishes. It results in the slow erosion of the finish or wood. It includes the mechanical or chemical disintegration and discoloration of the surface of wood that is caused by exposure to light, the action of dust and sand carried by winds, and the alternate shrinking and swelling of the surface fibers with the continual variation in, moisture content brought by changes in the weather. Weathering does not include decay. See Photochemical degradation.

Wedge — Small spacers used to ventilate moisture-prone siding. They are usually 1/8-inch thick and are driven in at the nailing location.

INDEX

Pages with illustrations have their numbers in *italics*. Pages with tables have their numbers in **bold**.

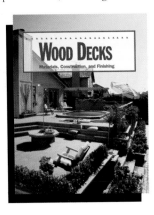